D0846640

HANOI &
HALONG BAY
ENCOUNTER

TOM DOWNS

Hanoi & Halong Bay Encounter

Published by Lonely Planet Publications Pty Ltd
ABN 36 005 607 983

Australia	Head Office, Locked Bag 1, Footscray, Vic 3011 ☎ 03 8379 8000 fax 03 8379 8111 talk2us@lonelyplanet.com.au
USA	150 Linden St, Oakland, CA 94607 ☎ 510 893 8555 toll free 800 275 8555 fax 510 893 8572 info@lonelyplanet.com
UK	72–82 Rosebery Ave, Clerkenwell, London EC1R 4RW ☎ 020 7841 9000 fax 020 7841 9001 go@lonelyplanet.co.uk

This title was commissioned in Lonely Planet's Melbourne office and produced by: **Commissioning Editor** Tashi Wheeler **Coordinating Editors** Joanne Newell, Stephanie Pearson **Coordinating Cartographer** Helen Rowley **Layout Designer** Wibowo Rusli **Senior Editors** Katie Lynch, Helen Christinis **Managing Cartographers** Julie Sheridan, David Connolly **Assisting Cartographer** Jessica Deane **Cover Designer** Mik Ruff **Project Manager** Sarah Sloane **Series Designers** Nic Lehman, Wendy Wright **Language Content Coordinator** Quentin Frayne **Thanks to** Sally Darmody, Michelle Glynn, Laura Jane, Wayne Murphy, Paul Piaia, Vivek Wagle, Celia Wood

Cover photograph One of the most popular ways to get around in Hanoi – by bicycle, Gavin Hellier/Jon Arnold Images/Alamy. **Internal photographs** p46, p49, p60, p79, p80, p97, p128 by Tom Downs. All other photographs by Lonely Planet Images, and by Greg Elms except p26 Simon Foale; p27 Mason Florence; p28 Anders Blomqvist; p101 Anthony Plummer; p108 David Greedy; p113 Richard I'Anson; p116 Juliet Coombe.

All images are copyright of the photographers unless otherwise indicated. Many of the images in this guide are available for licensing from **Lonely Planet Images:** www.lonelyplanetimages.com.

ISBN 978 1 74179 092 4

Printed through Colorcraft Ltd, Hong Kong.
Printed in China

HOW TO USE THIS BOOK
Colour-Coding & Maps
Colour-coding is used for symbols on maps and in the text that they relate to (eg all eating venues on the maps and in the text are given a green knife-and-fork symbol). Each neighbourhood also gets its own colour, and this is used down the edge of the page and throughout that neighbourhood section.

Send us your feedback We love to hear from readers – your comments help make our books better. We read every word you send us, and we always guarantee that your feedback goes straight to the appropriate authors. The most useful submissions are rewarded with a free book. To send us your updates and find out about Lonely Planet events, newsletters and travel news visit our award-winning website: *lonelyplanet .com/contact*.

Note: We may edit, reproduce and incorporate your comments in Lonely Planet products such as guidebooks, websites and digital products, so let us know if you don't want your comments reproduced or your name acknowledged. For a copy of our privacy policy visit *lonelyplanet.com/privacy*.

TOM DOWNS

Tom began travelling to and writing about Vietnam in the mid-1990s, when he journeyed from the south to the north with his wife, Fawn, a native of Saigon. They have returned frequently since then, falling in love with Hanoi's *bun cha, bia hoi* stands and fine colonial buildings. Above all, Tom has grown fond of the people of Hanoi, appreciating their obvious pride as well as their wry humour. He regards Hanoi as a very livable city, but prefers the 'assault on the senses' he experiences when hitting the city's streets anew on each visit. Among other books, he is author  of Lonely Planet's *New Orleans* city guide. He lives in Oakland, California, with Fawn and their kids Mai, Lana and Liam.

TOM'S THANKS

Thanks to Dao Van Thang and Steve Mills for their generosity and valuable insight. Hoang Vinh Nam and Hoang Thi Minh Hong offered key perspectives on modern Hanoi. Thanks also to Norman Nickens, Molly Tan, Christina Wegs, Luong Hai Hoa, Nguyen Minh Thu, Mason Florence, Kate Hoffman and Delia Garcia. At Lonely Planet, I owe kegs of *bia hoi* to Tashi Wheeler, Julie Sheridan and Joanne Newell. All my love to Fawn.

THE PHOTOGRAPHER

Greg Elms has been a contributor to Lonely Planet for over 15 years. Armed with a Bachelor of Arts in Photography, Greg was a photographer's assistant for two years before embarking on a travel odyssey. He eventually settled down to a freelance career in Melbourne, and now works regularly for magazines, graphic designers, advertising agencies and, of course, book publishers such as Lonely Planet.

Getting around in style, Old Quarter

CONTENTS

THIS IS HANOI

Hanoi captivates with its beauty, and truly gets under your skin with its irrepressible vitality. The city – once named Thang Long, for a mythical 'soaring dragon' – is indeed rising, and the local population is clearly energised. The city's thrust forward is unavoidable and infectious.

Hanoi is rare among Asian capitals, for the city is forging ahead without obliterating all signs of its past. Central Hanoi is an architectural show stopper held together by wide, tree-lined boulevards and mazes of intriguing alleys. The French architectural legacy, which Hanoians have little reason to feel romantic about, is nevertheless valued here. After decades of neglect, the city's treasure trove of villas and colonial government buildings is being restored and put to inviting use – most notably in the French Quarter's accumulation of fine restaurants. The Old Quarter, an agglomeration of humble 'tube houses', has been declared a historic district to protect the city's oldest and most colourful enclave.

But Hanoians rarely slow down to admire the beauty of their city. Hanoi's appeal is greatly enhanced by the exuberance of its citizens, the vast majority of whom seem to be whirring around the city on motorbikes. Hanoians have a reputation for regarding foreigners coldly, but most respond warmly to a smile. In increasing numbers, they are growing accustomed to doing business globally. Many are growing wealthy on the local stock market. All over town are signs of Hanoians enjoying the good life, and many are eager to share their thoughts and a toast with new friends from abroad.

This is an exciting time to visit Hanoi. The city is changing fast, but it offers an enticing blend of past and present. The arts, fashion and fine-dining scenes are flourishing as local talents and entrepreneurs respond to looser government control and growing opportunities. Meanwhile, traditional charms like a walk around Hoan Kiem Lake, or a bowl of *bun cha* (rice vermicelli with barbecued pork and vegetables) at an old woman's food stall, are to be savoured as much as ever.

Top left Traditional music accompanies the show at Thang Long Water Puppet Theatre (p55) **Top right** Artwork beside Hoan Kiem Lake depicts a myth associated with the lake (p58) **Bottom** Catching up over a *bia hoi* at Lan Chin (p78)

Bia Hoi Corner (p18) at night

>1 HO CHI MINH

PAYING RESPECTS TO UNCLE HO – IN PERSON

Commie economics have been thoroughly trounced in Vietnam, but Ho Chi Minh remains a revered national hero. Each year thousands of Vietnamese make the pilgrimage to see Bac Ho (Uncle Ho), and thousands of foreigners join them. Yes, after his death in 1969, Ho joined the pantheon of communist heroes and was embalmed. (Lenin and Mao also are embalmed.) Ho's body lies eternally in state in a formidable mausoleum (p84; pictured right) just off Ba Dinh Sq.

Seeing so historic a figure in the flesh can be surreal and also a little surprising. Nothing can really prepare you for it. It's plain to see that the man's physical stature is no match for the importance of his actions or the extent of his influence – for, although Vietnam is a smallish country, Ho (as the leader of its independence movement) found himself at the crux of one of the defining events of the latter half of the 20th century.

A visit to the mausoleum is naturally heightened if it coincides with the arrival of a bus-load of Vietnamese from the countryside, for whom the sight of their nation's father may have a spine-tingling effect. Adding to the gravity of the scene – and reminding us that Vietnam is still ruled by an authoritarian communist government – is the presence of military police, posted at intervals of five paces.

After your 'audience' with Uncle Ho, blaze your own Ho Chi Minh trail by visiting the provocative Ho Chi Minh Museum (p84), his elegant, though humble, stilt house (p84), and the Museum of Independence (p44).

HO QUICK SKETCH

He was born Nguyen Tat Thanh in 1890. His father was a nationalistic scholar. From 1911 to 1941 he travelled widely, including to France, England, the US, the Soviet Union and China. He joined the Communist Party in Paris in the 1920s. He furthered his education in Moscow and in Goangzhou, where he organised with other Vietnamese nationalists. In 1941 he became leader of the Vietnamese independence movement, and was named prime minister in 1945. He was president of North Vietnam from 1955 to 1969. He had many aliases, all of which had significant meaning. The one he settled on means 'enlightened will'.

>2 ART GALLERIES

SURVIVING A HANOI ART ATTACK

Hanoi challenges the notion that you can never have too much art. It seems the sale of a few paintings some years back resulted in a proliferation of promising new artists, and galleries galore. On the surface it's a very commercial movement, but the contemporary scene has garnered international attention over the past two decades.

The French kick-started things in 1925, when the Ecole des Beaux-Arts d'Indochine was founded here. The communists encouraged socialist realism and patriotic themes. Postmodernism arrived during the 1990s. Today, tourists seem to favour romantic Old Quarter scenes (jarringly motorbike-free) and portraits of nude women. Uniquely Vietnamese is the prevalent use of lacquer paint and silk canvases.

As you peruse the galleries, some motifs and styles will become familiar, but the true works of art will assert their presence. Some galleries are more commercial than others, but all are worth a look. Formally attired shopkeepers will guide you up several flights of stairs and through little rooms cluttered with hidden gems. Stroll along Pho Hang Gai and Pho Hang Bong (for both streets, see Map pp42–3, D5) in the Old Quarter, where at least two dozen shops don't just sell paintings, but overflow with them. Standout galleries in the Old Quarter include Apricot Gallery (p44; pictured right) and Mai Gallery (p47). Things are a little more low-key in the Nha Tho area

MASTERPIECES FOR CHEAPSKATES

In studios along Hang Trong, in the Nha Tho area, counterfeit artists knock out copies of the masters and sell them dirt cheap. For a mere US$35 to US$50 you can have a vibrant copy, rendered in oils, of Edward Hopper's *Nighthawks*, Leonardo's *Mona Lisa* or any of Botero's sombre studies of obesity. These copies fall short of the real thing, but beat crummy posters any day of the week.

Bring along a flattering photo of yourself and you can have your portrait painted. Who knows, maybe your smiling mug will be auctioned off in an estate sale 100 years from now. And, if your ego's running amok, you might also have yourself painted into a Picasso — or even a Botero.

(Map p57, B3) and along Trang Tien (Map pp68–9, D3) in the French Quarter. In the mix are galleries specialising in contemporary works by artists less interested in the tourist market. Make sure you check out Oriental Gallery (p61) in the Nha Tho area, and Dong Phong Art Gallery (p72) in the French Quarter. Perhaps Hanoi's finest art gallery is Art Vietnam (p96) in the West Lake area.

The casual art collector who doesn't ordinarily haunt galleries in the West will find Hanoi particularly rewarding. Fine works are relatively inexpensive, and foreigners are automatically regarded as a serious patrons of the arts. It's very flattering. Accommodating gallery owners will often go out of their way to arrange studio visits.

A quick education on local art history can be gained by spending a few hours at the Vietnam Fine Arts Museum (p90), which is not to be missed even if you intend skipping the gallery scene.

>3 TO MARKET
SHOPPING WITH THE HOI POLLOI OF HANOI

From a sightseeing perspective, the traditional public markets are endlessly interesting. They may one day be a thing of the past, though, as a growing number of Hanoians turns to malls and supermarkets for their shopping needs.

A tour of the markets must begin with Dong Xuan Market (p41; pictured above) in the Old Quarter. As Hanoi's largest covered market, it's a sprawling, three-level job that covers two city blocks. It's not beautiful, although the façade dates back to 1889, and a visit doesn't qualify as a shopping spree so much as a cultural experience. The market is refreshingly geared towards low-income locals rather than tourists. Merchandise spills out of the stalls and into the aisles, causing pedestrian gridlock as shoppers attempt to squeeze through. Interesting stuff sold here includes dried-fruit sweets, conical hats, handbags, berets, dried shrimp, dried squid, dainty face-masks for motorbike riders, ubercute clothing for pampered children and trendy jackets for

anyone who didn't read up on the local climate before a winter trip. The top two levels are given over almost exclusively to tailors and the local garment industry. You might have 'em cut that pinstriped Capone suit you've always wanted, and they'll probably do it for a song.

Dong Xuan's lack of fresh food items is more than compensated for at the nearby Pho Gia Ngu market (see the boxed text, p44). Here you'll find buckets filled with live fish, crabs, clams, eels, frogs and prawns. Better still, many vendors sell fresh tropical fruits – rambutans, mangoes, durians and other treats. Or just slide into a table and order a bowl of noodles, a plate of roast pigeon or the grimacing snout of a roasted dog. On Friday and Saturday nights, a huge night market (p44) takes over several blocks of the Old Quarter, centring on Hang Duong. The market mostly deals in cheap knock-off goods from China: stickers with which to decorate your mobile phone, slippers as cute as puppies, fake designer jeans, fake Pumas (or 'Pamus') and whatnot. It's quite an occasion, as Hanoi's working class take to the streets in great numbers to test their purchasing power. It's good fun to join in.

>4 LANGUAGE LESSONS

HAVING A GO AT THE LINGO

Vietnamese is not an easy language to learn, and you're probably not going to get very far with it in a visit of only a few days. Even so, putting your tongue to the test can be a fun way to break the ice with the local people. It adds a personable spin to the usual range of transactions you are likely to have during your stay.

Vietnamese is a tonal language. Speaking it requires discipline akin to precisely hitting the notes of a song. Get the tone wrong and a polite greeting can be transformed into an embarrassing faux pas. However, your efforts are likely to be appreciated by Hanoians, who are, by and large, good-natured people. A little self-deprecating humour goes a long way. Resign yourself to this, because your bad accent is guaranteed to make people laugh.

Young Vietnamese are always approaching tourists with stuff they're trying to sell – counterfeit books, postcards, cheap souvenirs. You might as well get something out of the exchange by practising your Vietnamese on them. They can actually be fun to talk to, these street-smart kids. They'll freely correct your Vietnamese, teach you some current slang and share some insight on life in Hanoi.

A handy tool to have is Lonely Planet's *Vietnamese Phrasebook*. Or check out p146 for a rundown of useful Vietnamese terms. Additionally, carry your own little notebook to jot down useful phrases gathered along the way. Hanoians can be nosy people, so anytime you're spotted writing notes you'll attract attention. A perfect stranger is likely to approach and ask, 'What are you doing?' Your reply in clumsy Vietnamese is likely to replace suspicion with a smile.

>5 BIA HOI CORNER

SWILLING CHEAP BEER ON AN ANKLE-HIGH STOOL

Rush hour on the Bia Hoi Corner (at the intersection of Pho Ta Hien and Pho Luong Ngoc Quyen in the Old Quarter – see Map pp42–3, E3) is one of Hanoi's unique and unexpected offerings. Three *bia hoi* (draught beer) joints set up tiny plastic stools on the kerbs and serve crap beer from kegs, while the frenetic Old Quarter provides the entertainment just by being itself. The crossroads here is particularly conducive to people-watching, and the price of a beer – around 2000d per glass – means you and your friends can wet your tonsils just about free of charge.

The people-watching is never dull. It's a live show, with no rehearsal, no direction, and usually no real consideration for the audience. Street musicians sometimes sing mournful tunes through the cheapest of speakers, and a retinue of hustlers will try to charm you out of 10,000d or so. The beer and your low-lying vantage point somehow make everything seem larger than life. Between the bad brew and the motorbike fumes you're guaranteed a nasty headache in the morning unless you move on after a few rounds, but the experience is definitely something to write home about. For more on the brew that is *bia hoi*, see the boxed text, p52.

>6 GOURMET RESTAURANTS

DINING FINE, IN LUXURY

The French colonialists were given an indecorous send-off in 1954. Their villas, however, were lovingly preserved, and today many house fine restaurants frequented by French tourists as well as visitors from other countries. Surely this irony is not lost on the Vietnamese, who will work in these places but seem not to dine there (although many can afford to). These villa-restaurants offer exquisite atmosphere and sophisticated Asian cuisine. Plan on having a romantic meal at Club 51 (p74; pictured above), the Emperor (p75), Au Lac House (p73), Green Tangerine (p50) or Le Tonkin (p76).

Not all of Hanoi's high-end eateries hark back to 1953, though. Vine (p99), near West Lake, is exceedingly popular, serves excellent food and has the city's best wine selection. It's very much in step with contemporary Hanoi. Reflecting Hanoi's increasingly cosmopolitan tastes, Restaurant Bobby Chinn (p77) brings together flamboyant atmosphere and smart East-West cuisine.

You're on holiday, so (literally) loosen your belt a few notches and enjoy the best Hanoi has to offer.

>7 STREET FOOD
CHOWING DOWN AT STREET STALLS

If you're seriously into food, and want to experience the best that Hanoi has to offer, there's no getting around the street stalls. There may be no getting around them anyway, if you're trying to walk down a pavement that's cluttered with vendors, their pots and their customers parked on little plastic stools.

The cuisine of Hanoi was born on the pavements, where (mostly) women cooks do just one thing all day, every day. As they say, practice makes perfect. You choose where you eat based on what you're craving, whether you fancy *bun cha* (rice vermicelli with barbecued pork and vegetables), *banh cuon* (silky steamed rice crepes filled with minced pork, mushrooms and ground shrimp), rice plates, bowls of noodles, seafood or *banh mi* (fresh French bread).

If dining a few inches above the pavement isn't your style, the same calibre of cooking is offered in countless one-dish indoor eateries, particularly in the Old Quarter, where stark, subsidy-era atmosphere emphasises that it's really all about the food. For great one-dish eats, check out Cha Ca La Vong (p48; pictured above), Bun Cha Nem Ran (p48) and Banh Ghoi (p62). Our dining recommendations in the neighbourhood chapters include these and many other favourites, but mercilessly leave out hundreds of undiscovered culinary delights. If you've come to enjoy the unrestrained flavours of Vietnam, you're sure to find your personal nirvana.

>8 ETHNIC MINORITIES

IMMERSING YOURSELF IN MINORITY CULTURE

Vietnam is home to 54 ethnic groups, including the Kinh (Viet) majority. Many of the smaller groups live in isolated mountain communities and retain traditional lifestyles. Some have attracted much international interest for their intricately woven textiles and for their unique architecture. If you have several extra days, head for Sapa (see the boxed text, p87), where minority groups congregate at the markets. But if you haven't the time for such an excursion, you can get an introduction to these fascinating cultures without leaving Hanoi.

The excellent Vietnam Fine Arts Museum (p90) has a finely presented exhibit of ethnic crafts, textiles and clothing, and more of the same is on view at the Museum of Vietnamese Women (p71). The Vietnam Museum of Ethnology (p86) has a comprehensive collection of minority crafts, as well as displays explaining cultural traditions and celebrations. In the museum's backyard you can nose around amid some awesome ethnic structures.

Ethnic textiles make for beautiful souvenirs, but not all textiles are authentic. Head to shops like Craftlink (p90), which sells garments produced exclusively by ethnic women. Craftlink's mission is to ensure the craftspeople receive their fair share of the profits. Antique fabrics and arts are sold at 54 Traditions Gallery (p96; pictured above), which is well worth a visit even if you're not in a buying mood.

>9 HOAN KIEM LAKE

PROMENADING AROUND HANOI'S FAVOURITE LAKE

In the heart of Hanoi, Hoan Kiem Lake (Map p57, C3) is a serene and scenic oval that begs to be circumnavigated. A walk around its shaded, paved paths ought to take less than an hour, allowing time to admire French-colonial architecture and to stop for a quick coffee at the Hapro Coffee Kiosk (p64).

The lake shows its truest colours in the wee hours of the morning, when Hanoians observe their daily exercise rituals, running and walking laps around the water. It begins around 5am, before the sun is up, and before the air is choked with motorbike exhaust. A steady stream of humanity flows around the lake until about 7am, when government loudspeakers begin to blare patriotic music to rouse the working masses. In the mix are callisthenic brigades partaking in an interesting t'ai chi–Jazzercize hybrid. If you're jet-lagging, who knows, maybe you'll be up at this hour. Join 'em.

On sultry evenings, it can seem like all of Hanoi is cooling off on motorbikes circling around the lake. Makes more sense than sitting still in your air-con hotel room. Flag down your friendly *xe om* (motorbike taxi) driver for a few circuits.

>10 XE OM HIGH JINKS
HUGGING THE CURVES ON A MOTORBIKE TAXI

Pack 100 cars into a city block and you have gridlock, but that many motorbikes will flow right along. They are noisy and the exhaust is undeniably bad for your health, but motorbikes make sense in Hanoi. The city's constant, groaning traffic moves around town like tightly packed schools of fish. The tourist walking the pavement may well feel the urge to get into the stream of things, and indeed a spin around town is exhilarating and, frankly, addictive.

However, driving in Hanoi traffic is dangerous for the neophyte. It's far wiser to hop aboard someone else's motorbike, and this is easily arranged. *Xe om* (pronounced say-*ome*), roughly translated, means 'motorbike hug', but for all practical purposes it means 'motorbike taxi'. You don't really have to hug your driver. On nearly every corner of the city you'll find about three *xe om* drivers, and if you're walking by they'll offer their services. Some are old soldiers and some are roguish young men, but most are polite and even a little sheepish in making their pitch. These guys are unlicensed and basically unemployed, but the vast majority are honest and it's perfectly legal to hire them. Cross your fingers and hope you've chosen well, because you're putting your life in their hands. Find someone you like and you may be able to hire him as a chauffeur for the duration of your trip. See the boxed text, p144, for tips on negotiating fares.

>11 SILKS & CERAMICS

TREATING YOURSELF TO GRACE AND ELEGANCE

For some, travel is an opportunity to purchase items not available back home, and even in this globalised day and age Hanoi offers a bounty of unique and special products. Top of the list is silk. Vietnamese silk is not necessarily the world's finest, but the Vietnamese fashion sense is colourful, fun and graceful to the point of ethereality. The market here is primarily geared towards women seeking snazzy shirts, flowery scarves and traditional *ao dai* (Vietnamese national dress). But men are certainly not excluded. Ties and shirts abound, and even macho world leaders George Bush and Vladimir Putin donned *ao dai* while in Hanoi for an economic summit in 2006. You will find silk shops galore along Pho Hang Gai and Pho Hang Bong (for both streets, see Map pp42–3, D5) in the Old Quarter, and silk fashions are also sold in boutiques around Nha Tho (Map p57, B3). Check out Cocoon (p58), Kenly Silk (p47) and Khaisilk (p47).

Vietnamese ceramics are also worth inspecting. Teapots, buddhas and candleholders come in a variety of elegant styles. Shops sell ceramics all over town, but the shops of Nha Tho feature artistic modern designs – see Marena, p59. For old-world flavour, head to Phuong Dong Art Shop (p61).

HIGHLIGHTS

>12 WATER PUPPETS

GAZING IN AWE AT ASTOUNDING WATER PUPPETRY

Water puppetry is a uniquely Vietnamese form of entertainment that brings together drama, live music and occasional pyrotechnics over a stage that is, essentially, a large wading pool. The city's world-renowned water-puppet troupes are likely to travel through your home country about as frequently as Haley's Comet passes overhead, so the smart thing to do is to catch a show while you're in town.

The tradition is believed to have begun in the Red River Delta, near Hanoi, over 1000 years ago. Very likely its first practitioners were rice farmers accustomed to spending much of their time waist-deep in the rice paddies. The puppeteers wade behind a bamboo screen, operating brilliantly painted wooden puppets with nylon strings and wooden poles. Vignettes relate Vietnamese myths and legends.

The music is performed by a traditional Vietnamese orchestra stationed on terra firma, to the side of the water stage. The compositions are intricately arranged and at times mesmerising.

See p55 for information on performances at the Thang Long Water Puppet Theatre, the best and most central venue for this unique art form.

>13 HALONG BAY

SETTING SAIL ON EMERALD WATERS

No doubt you've heard it all before, but Halong Bay (p101) really is a wonder to behold. Some 3000 islands – limestone formations, actually – roll like camels' humps out of the bay's emerald waters. In the bay's secluded sanctuaries, the horizon in all directions is filled with rows of hillocks in shades of blue, grey and purple, depending on how near or far away they are. Halong Bay is about 2½ hours from Hanoi, making a day trip possible. It's a very long day, but it gets you out on the bay and back to your Hanoi hotel in time for bed.

Overnighting aboard an atmospheric 'junk' is the way to go, though. Boarding a boat with other travellers always has the ominous feeling that a five-year *Gilligan's Island* experience may be in the offing. But get past these reservations and you'll soon be dining and boozing with newfound boon companions, taking night swims in phosphorescent waters, and lying beneath the stars as your boat gently rocks you to sleep. The second day often includes activities such as kayaking, or hiking on Cat Ba Island (p104).

Many companies operate boats that depart from Halong City. Rather than sort through them all, just visit a reputable tour company (see p111) in Hanoi. Tours of one to three nights can easily be arranged as late as a day before you intend to set sail.

>HANOI DIARY

A smattering of national and religious holidays light up Hanoi's calendar. Some make a bigger splash than others, with Tet (Vietnamese New Year) being the daddy of them all. Spring and autumn are busy seasons, but very little goes down during the steamy summer months. Most of the religious festivals are older than the wind, so pinning down the dates is a matter of familiarising yourself with an ancient lunar calendar. A good Vietnamese calendar (which differs slightly from the Chinese calendar) is posted at www.informatik.uni-leipzig.de/~duc/amlich.

Bringing home a kumquat tree in preparation for Tet (Vietnamese New Year; p29)

HANOI DIARY

JANUARY

New Year's Day (Tet Duong Lich)
The first day of the Gregorian calendar (1 January) doesn't get nearly the same play as Tet, but buildings are emblazoned with red *'chuc mung nam moi'* (Happy New Year) signs.

Vietnamese New Year (Tet Nguyen Dan)
The big tomato on the Vietnamese calendar sees the city shut down for about a week in late January or February. (See the boxed text, opposite.)

FEBRUARY

Anniversary of the Founding of the Vietnamese Communist Party (Thanh Lap Dang)
This national holiday occurs on 3 February, commemorating the founding of the Vietnamese Communist Party on this day in 1930.

Lim Festival
In Lim Village, 18km from Hanoi, local singers perform the unusual Quan Ho folk songs at this festival, held on the 13th day after Tet.

Valentine's Day
The sappiest of Western holidays is gaining ground rapidly in Hanoi. The entire city swoons and just about turns pink every 14 February.

Dressing up for Tet Nguyen Dan, Hanoi's biggest festival

A FÊTE CALLED TET

Day One on the lunar calendar – called Tet Nguyen Dan, or simply Tet – is the biggest, busiest and noisiest of holidays. It is a time of new beginnings, when families spend time together peacefully, loose ends and debts are cleared up, the house is cleaned and anything representing bad luck is tucked away and forgotten about. During the build-up, the Old Quarter is ablaze with flowers and blossoming peach and kumquat trees, all of which are believed to bring good luck. Shops stock up on Tet staples such as *banh chung,* a little square cake made with fatty pork and bean paste. The festival itself begins on the first day of the year and lasts three days, with lots of deliberate noisemaking designed to ward off evil spirits. Many shops and businesses shut down for an entire week.

Tet falls between 19 January and 20 February, depending on how the lunar and solar (Western) calendars line up. It's a very busy travel time, as thousands of overseas Vietnamese fly home for the holiday.

MARCH

Hai Ba Trung Festival

A parade on the sixth day of the second lunar month celebrates the heroics of the two Trung Sisters, who led an uprising against the Chinese in AD 40.

Perfume Pagoda Pilgrimage

On the full moon of the second lunar month, thousands trek to a temple in a mountain cave, 60km southwest of Hanoi, for Vietnam's biggest Buddhist pilgrimage.

APRIL

Le Mat Snake Festival

On the 23rd day of the third lunar month, a village 6km east of Hanoi goes mad for snakes, with processions, music, drama and *ruou* (rice wine) infused with snake blood.

Liberation Day (Saigon Giai Phong)

The liberation of Saigon (30 April 1975) is commemorated all over the country. It's coupled with Workers' Day, for a two-day break.

MAY

International Workers' Day

Held on 1 May, it's a national holiday, which (in theory) means workers get the day off.

Ho Chi Minh's Birthday (Sinh Nhat Bac Ho)

The anniversary of Uncle Ho's birth (19 May 1890) is a national holiday. Birthday cakes with lighted candles are not permitted inside the mausoleum, however.

JUNE

Children's Day

A national holiday, on 1 June, honours young Vietnamese.

Buddha's Birthday (Phat Dan)

Buddha's birthday, on the eighth day of the fourth moon (usually June), brings splashes of light as lanterns are hung outside pagodas and some private homes.

AUGUST

Wandering Souls Day (Trung Nguyen)

The Vietnamese equivalent of All Souls Day is celebrated with offerings to 'wandering souls'. Held on the full moon of the seventh lunar month, it's a time of forgiveness and for cleaning the graveyards.

SEPTEMBER

National Day (Quoc Khanh)

This commemorates the 2 September 1945 proclamation of the Declaration of Independence. Look for fireworks on Ba Dinh Sq (Map p83, C2) and boat races on Hoan Kiem Lake (Map p57, C3).

Mid-Autumn Festival (Trung Tu)

On the full moon of the eighth lunar month (September or October), shops are stocked with sweets and cakes, and festival eve is lit up by colourful lanterns.

DECEMBER

Christmas Day (Giang Sinh)

Christmas (25 December) is becoming popular in Hanoi as spangly displays light up the malls and Santa whirls around town on his motorbike.

Time out for tea in the Old Quarter

ITINERARIES

If you have just one day, or two, or three, narrowing down Hanoi's sights and amusements to the essentials isn't too tricky, but it helps to have some pointers. Our suggestions will get you started.

DAY ONE

Start with a morning constitutional around Hoan Kiem Lake (p22). Get out there early enough and you'll be joining a steady stream of locals exercising before work. Stop along the way for coffee at lakeside Hapro Coffee Kiosk (p64), then wander the Old Quarter's maze of narrow streets and shops. Be sure to walk down Pho Hang Bac (Map pp42–3, E4), where chisellers carve names onto headstones, through imposing Dong Xuan Market (p41), and through the Pho Gia Ngu food market (see the boxed text, p44). See the preserved 19th-century house at 87 Pho Ma May (p41), once the home of local merchants, and the tiny Museum of Independence (p44). Pick a spot for a casual Vietnamese lunch, then check out the silk shops and art galleries along Pho Hang Gai (Map pp42–3, D5) and Pho Hang Bong (Map pp42–3, D5). Have an extravagant dinner at Club 51 (p74) and cool off with a drink at Hanoi Cinemateque (p81).

DAY TWO

Start with a bowl of hearty *pho* (rice-noodle soup). To see Ho Chi Minh, Vietnam's embalmed national hero, go to the Ho Chi Minh Mausoleum (p84) early (last entry is at 10.15am), then have a look at Ho's humble stilt house (p84). Get over to the Nha Tho area for a look at the historic Hanoi Cathedral (p58) and to shop at some of Hanoi's finest galleries and boutiques (see p58). Have lunch at the superb La Salsa (p63) tapas bar and catch a cab out to the engrossing Vietnam Museum of Ethnology (p86) to get acquainted with the cultures of Vietnam's diverse ethnic groups. In the early evening, park on a stool at the Old Quarter's Bia Hoi Corner (p18), and have dinner at Highway 4 (p51) or Green Tangerine (p50). At night, see the water puppets at Thang Long Water Puppet Theatre (p55).

Top left Get a caffeine boost at Hapro Coffee Kiosk (p64), beside Hoan Kiem Lake **Top right** Traditional dancers at Hoan Kiem Lake **Bottom** At the end of a long Hanoi day, cool off with a drink at the bar at I-Box restaurant (p62)

DAY THREE

Devote day three to Hanoi's high culture. After a leisurely coffee at Cafe Pho Co (p53), beat the tour buses by getting to the Temple of Literature (p90) early. Reserve time for a massage at Maison des Artes (p93). Have lunch at the honourable KOTO (p92) and then spend a couple of hours at the Vietnam Fine Arts Museum (p90). Thus inspired, peruse the art galleries and shops along Pho Trang Tien (Map pp68–9, D3) in the French Quarter, and have dinner at the splendorous Emperor (p75) or relaxed Le Tonkin (p76). Indulge in a decadent nightcap at Le Club champagne bar (p78) in the Metropole Hotel.

DAY FOUR

If you have four full days, scrap the day-three plan and devote two days to Halong Bay (p101), with a night aboard a boat. Whether you opt for a high-class five-star cruise ship or a more humble 'junk', you're guaranteed an unforgettable, once-in-a-lifetime experience that can involve night swimming in the bay's phosphorescent waters, kayaking, hiking, and drinking wine and beer with your shipmates into the wee hours. One-night tours generally depart early in the morning and get you back to Hanoi in time for dinner the next day. You may not feel like having another big night, but get out for a last helping of *bun cha* (rice vermicelli

FORWARD PLANNING

Some of the pleasures of travel cannot be planned, but some things are best taken care of beforehand. In Vietnam's case, a few important details absolutely must be settled before you leave home.

Four weeks before you go After you have bought your airline tickets, you'll need to apply for an entry visa through the nearest Vietnamese consulate. See p141 for details. Around the same time, it's a good idea to start figuring out your accommodations. During some holidays (Tet, in particular) hotels are more likely to fill up early, so be aware of the local calendar (see p27). Many websites provide photos of hotels and assist with booking – for more information on accommodation in Hanoi, see p120.

Two weeks before you go If you're not going to be in Hanoi long, it's a good idea to familiarise yourself with the local restaurant and food-stall scene. It helps to have an idea of what dishes you want to try and to know where you can get them. It's also wise to reserve tables at some of the snazzier French Quarter restaurants.

The day before you go Reconfirm your flight. Pack your eye mask. Phone your parents to say goodbye.

with barbecued pork and vegetables) and another round at a *bia hoi* (draught beer) joint. Or treat yourself to a special meal at Vine (p99).

RAINY DAY

If you're in town during spring, you'll have to get used to Hanoi's persistent drizzle. Locals call it *mua bui* or *mua phun* (rain dust), and they don't let it interfere with their outdoor activities. Try to do the same. In summer you may experience some very wet days, making strolls through the Old Quarter more of a slog. Thankfully, Hanoi is a museum-happy city, so you'll have plenty of indoor options. On Monday, when the museums all close, grab an umbrella and spend the day gallery-hopping and shopping along Pho Hang Gai (Map pp42–3, D5), Pho Hang Bong (Map pp42–3, D5), Pho Nha Tho (Map p57, B3), Pho Nha Chung (Map p57, B4) and Pho Trang Tien (Map pp68–9, D3). See a water-puppet show at Thang Long Water Puppet Theatre (p55), where the performers are wetter than you. To get around, take advantage of the city's growing fleet of taxis.

> NEIGHBOURHOODS

Motorbikes: love 'em or hate 'em, it's hard to ignore 'em

NEIGHBOURHOODS

NEIGHBOURHOODS

Most travellers to Hanoi have just a few days to experience the best the city has to offer. Fortunately, Hanoi is fairly compact, with most of its central neighbourhoods within a walkable area – or only a short ride away on the back of a motorbike.

Take a walk around lovely Hoan Kiem Lake and you'll get a pretty good idea of how Hanoi fits together. Above the lake is the Old Quarter, with its jumble of crooked lanes, tightly packed shops and backpacker hotels. You'll want to spend at least a day and an evening experiencing the Old Quarter's ancient architecture, markets, food stalls and *bia hoi* (draught beer) joints. Let your curiosity and your appetite guide you, and just assume you'll get lost.

West of Hoan Kiem Lake, Pho Nha Tho anchors a burgeoning fashion district that's hopping with boutiques, art shops and international restaurants. An adjunct to this strip is Hanoi's bustling backpacker ghetto, Pho Hang Hanh – a curvy street crammed with hip bars, cheap eats and inexpensive flops.

Below the lake and to the east is the French Quarter, a grid of wide-open thoroughfares lined with art galleries and colonial villas that are now occupied by some of Hanoi's finest restaurants. Many of the official buildings left behind by the French have been converted into museums. Immediately to the south, the Hai Ba Trung District also offers refined dining.

A little to the west of the French Quarter is the Dong Da area, attracting culture vultures with its landmark Temple of Literature. When you're ready to see Ho Chi Minh, head north to the Ho-saturated Ba Dinh district – it's home to the Ho Chi Minh Mausoleum complex, where Vietnam's greatest hero is preserved for public viewing.

Gallery-hoppers will want to venture above the Old Quarter, into the Truc Bach and West Lake area. The secluded island community of Ngu Xa is good for a stroll and a bite to eat.

With an adventurous spirit, you'll get to know your way around this beautiful city in just a few days.

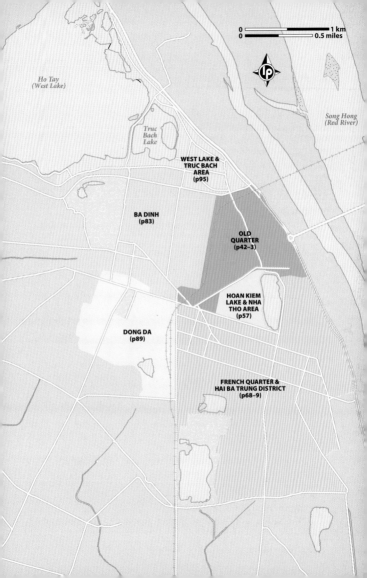

>OLD QUARTER

The Old Quarter is indeed old, with more than 1000 years of history, but the neighbourhood is really a stirring blend of past and present. It's a jumble of ancient buildings blurred behind a 21st-century pace of life. There's no such thing as a leisurely stroll down its densely packed lanes, each curving and changing shape from block to block. Along Pho Hang Bac, tombstones are stacked high from door to door, while down Pho Lo Ren a dozen noisy welders ply their trade. The pavements disappear beneath parked motorbikes, food vendors and the merchandise that overflows from tiny shops. The streets swarm with agile two-wheelers, clunkier *cyclos* (pedicabs or bicycle rickshaws) and old women carrying yokes weighted by hefty pots. While tourism is thriving in this part of town, it is dwarfed by the local commerce, and you're sure to get lost wandering the Old Quarter's maze of fascinating streets.

OLD QUARTER

◉ SEE
87 Ma May	1	F4
Bach Ma Temple	2	E3
Dong Xuan Market	3	E2
Museum of Independence	4	E3
Night Market	5	E2

🏠 SHOP
Apricot Gallery	6	D5
Codo Gallery	7	D5
F Silk	8	E5
Hanoi Gallery	9	E3
Hieu Phuc Loi	10	E3
Ho Guom Audio	11	D4
Kenly Silk	12	D5
Khaisilk	13	D5
Mai Gallery	14	C6
Thang Long Gallery	15	E4

🍴 EAT
Banh Cuon Gia Truyen	16	C3
Bun Cha Nem Ran	17	E3
Cha Ca La Vong	18	D3
Cha Ca Thanh Long	19	C4
Green Tangerine	20	F4
Highway 4	21	G4
Nha Hang Phu My	22	C4
Pho Gia Truyen	23	C4
Tamarind Café	24	F3

🍸 DRINK
Bia Hoi 68 Hang Quat	25	D4
Cafe Giang	26	E4
Cafe Lam	27	F4
Cafe Pho Co	28	E5
Cafe Ruou (Walker's Pub)	29	D4
Legends Beer	30	E4
Mao's Red Lounge	31	E3
O Quan Chuong	32	E2
Quan Bia Minh	33	E4
Red Beer	34	F4

⭐ PLAY
Ho Guom Audio	(see 11)	
Jazz Club Minh	35	E4
Thang Long Water Puppet Theatre	36	F5

Please see over for map

SEE

87 MA MAY
☎ 928 5604; 87 Pho Ma May; admission 5000d; ⏰ 9-11am & 2-5pm

The traditional houses of the Old Quarter are a huge part of the neighbourhood's appeal, but you'll rarely have an opportunity to see beyond their shopfronts. Here, you can – and this house is a beauty, lovingly restored and frozen in its late-19th-century condition. The woodwork upstairs is particularly impressive, and it's surprising to see how effectively the courtyard creates an open, livable space.

BACH MA TEMPLE
76 Pho Hang Buom; donations accepted; ⏰ 7-11am & 2-5pm

Tiny Bach Ma is Hanoi's oldest place of worship, having been established early in the 11th century by city founder Emperor Ly Thai To. A horse statue in the temple honours a legendary steed that is said to have helped the emperor establish the nearby citadel. Much of the existing temple resulted from an 1839 restoration. Resistance fighters hid out here during the French period.

DONG XUAN MARKET
Cau Dong; ⏰ 6am-midnight

It's hard to miss the Old Quarter's sprawling, three-level market – and nor should you try. It's a fascinating, ramshackle market that's refreshingly geared towards local shoppers, rather than tourists. The market isn't necessarily the best place to hunt for curios; a visit is more of a cultural experience than a shopping excursion. See also p15.

DEEP IN THE OLD QUARTER

Like most residences in the Old Quarter, the house at 87 Pho Ma May is a tube house – long and narrow with a shop open to the street and private living quarters to the rear and upstairs. Houses like this were cleverly squeezed into slim lots to cheat an ancient system that calculated property taxes in proportion to a property's width. A visit to 87 Pho Ma May is culturally interesting, but the house feels somewhat devoid of life. To observe more, just follow business signs (internet cafés, coffee shops etc) that point into those dark tunnels between houses. Some of these passages are meandering labyrinths leading to hidden doors and stairways, and walking through them can afford a somewhat voyeuristic glimpse into Old Quarter life. There's no need to make your curiosity obvious; just make your way to the business you're looking for, and try to grasp the density of the neighbourhood along the way.

E F G H

1

Long
Bien

Đ Yen Phu

400 m
0.2 miles

2

Nguyen Cao Thang
P Thanh Ha
32
P Hang Chieu
Nguyen Sieu
P Phuc Tan
Đ Tran Nhat Duat

3

To Le Mat
Snake Village
(6km)
Chuong Doung Bridge

2
Dao Duy Tu
10
P Ta Hien
31
P Luong Ngoc Quyen
17
24
Handspan
34
1
P Ma May
Hang Muoi
P Nguyen Huu Huan
Hang Tre

9
4
P Hang Ngang
P Hang Bac
P Luong Van Can

35
Hang Dao
P Gia Ngu
33
P Hang Be
27
21
P Bach Dang

4

15
26
30
P Dinh Liet
20
P Cau Go
Hapro Tourist
Information Centre
P Dinh Tien Hoang
36
Lo Su
Hang Thung

28
P Hang Hanh
P Bao Khanh
The Huc
Bridge
P Hang Dau
P Ly Thai To

5

Đ Tran Quang Khai

P Trong Trong
P Le Thai To
Nha Tho
HOAN KIEM LAKE &
NHA THO AREA
Hoan Kiem Lake
Tran Nguyen Han
P Dinh Tien Hoang
P Tong Dan

6

P Nha Chung
Le Lai
FRENCH QUARTER

🅒 MUSEUM OF INDEPENDENCE

48 Pho Hang Ngang; admission free; 🕐 8-11.30am & 2-4.30pm

The small Old Quarter house where Ho Chi Minh lived in 1945 has been converted into a museum. Ho drafted the Declaration of Independence while living and working here. The exhibit of photos on the ground floor is worth a quick look, as are Ho's upstairs living quarters, where you can soak in the frozen-in-time feel of the place. See also p10.

🅒 NIGHT MARKET

Pho Dong Xuan, Pho Hang Duong & Pho Hang Ngang; 🕐 8pm-midnight Fri & Sat

The outdoor Night Market is very different from the workaday Dong Xuan (p41), mostly because it's more of a social event. Locals stroll the streets shoulder to shoulder as they peruse inexpensive goods for sale at the lighted stalls. It's fun and colourful, and definitely not about the shopping.

🛍 SHOP

🅒 APRICOT GALLERY *Art*

☎ 828 8965; www.apricot-artvietnam .com; 40B Pho Hang Bong; 🕐 8am-8pm

Many of Hanoi's most accomplished contemporary artists are shown at this immense, multi-storey gallery. You're also likely

---

STREETS OF THE OLD QUARTER

Sightseeing in the compact and congested Old Quarter is an irresistible walk-and-gawk sort of experience. Here's a rundown of some of the quarter's most interesting thoroughfares.

Pho Hang Gai (D5) Shops along this street sell beautifully designed silk goods. There are excellent art galleries as well.

Pho Gia Ngu (F4) A lively street market with food stalls and produce vendors fills the block day and night.

Pho Lo Ren (D3) An entire block of blacksmith shops rings and zaps with clanging and welding, most of it performed on the pavement.

Pho Hang Bac (E4) Several shops along here sell hand-chiselled tombstones. The corner shop at 99 Hang Bac showcases a headstone with Britney Spears' photo on it. Whenever you're ready for that, Britney, come on by and pick it up.

Nguyen Quang Bich (C4) The Old Quarter's beautiful, though somewhat decrepit, architecture is more easily appreciated here, where the houses lack bustling ground-floor shops.

Pho Hang Manh (D5) Many shops here sell traditional Vietnamese musical instruments, including gongs, *dan bau* (like a one-stringed steel guitar with a whammy bar), spike fiddles and percussive frogs that croak when you drag a mallet over their backs.

to encounter older works by local masters. A visit is an illuminating and highly hospitable experience.

CODO GALLERY *Art*
☎ 825 8573; www.codoartvietnam .com; 46 Pho Hang Bong; ☽ 8am-8pm
Refreshingly, not everything exhibited here appears to have been produced in the last year. The collection seems endless, with always another flight of stairs or an unopened door awaiting, but it's worth venturing all the way in. Some of the more intriguing, though perhaps less popular, works are hidden away.

F SILK *Fashion*
☎ 928 6786; fsilk@hn.vnn.vn; 82 Pho Hang Gai; ☽ 10am-7pm
If you're making the silk shop rounds, make sure you include this super shop, which has an endless selection of well-designed garments.

HANOI GALLERY *Art*
☎ 826 7850; 127 Pho Hang Buom; ☽ 9am-9pm
For half a century the Communist Party has been driving home its positive, nationalist message with artistic propaganda posters. You can still uncover appealing gems among this shop's well-picked-through collection of originals. Posters cost from US$50 to US$300.

WHAT'S WITH THE NAMES?
When Hanoi's 36 guilds established themselves here in the 13th century, the streets were named for the type of merchandise originally sold along them. The word *hang* means a business or shop, and is followed with a qualifier to indicate what product or service is provided within. Hence, Pho Hang Ga is 'chicken shop street' and Pho Hang Manh is 'bamboo-screen shop street'. Most (though not all) Old Quarter street names adhere to this name system. However, the nature of the businesses along most of the streets has evolved over the centuries, and no longer matches the street name. Exceptions are Pho Lo Ren (blacksmiths), Pho Hang Gai (silk shops) and Pho Cha Ca (grilled-fish eateries).

HIEU PHUC LOI
Wood-block stamps
☎ 928 0965; 2B Pho Ta Hien; ☽ 9am-9pm
Local watercolour artists all have their own stamp with which they sign their works. Such elegantly designed, personalised stamps can be purchased at cluttered little shops such as this one for 35,000d or more. The designs are hand-carved on wood blocks, and you'll get a red-ink stamp pad along with your purchase. Stick around to watch 'em make yours.

Nguyen Minh Thu
Tuoc lao *(bamboo water pipe) aficionado*

What are you smoking? It's tobacco grown in the northwest, in the mountains. **How much does it cost to have a hit on the pipe?** You buy the tobacco. It sells for 1000d. Smaller packets are 500d. **How does it make you feel when you smoke it?** I feel good. In the morning, when I wake up I smoke and feel better. First I smoke, then I brush my teeth. **Do you prefer the pipe to cigarettes?** Yes. Sometimes I smoke cigarettes, but cigarettes are not good for the health. If I smoke five cigarettes, I feel sick. But *tuoc lao* makes me feel OK. **I don't see many women smoking the pipe.** No, only old women in the countryside. **Do all ages smoke it?** Mostly people age 20 and up.

SMOKE ON THE WATER

The *tuoc lao* is a bamboo water pipe – a bong, basically – in which regular tobacco is smoked. You will see old men and young men in equal numbers taking deep drags on these things on pavements around Hanoi, usually at little makeshift tea stands. As smoke pours from their mouths and nostrils, the men shake their heads as though to help the nicotine reach the nether regions of their brains. It might appear to be excruciating, but most of these guys wax poetic about the pleasures of their addiction. If you're curious, you can ask a local to introduce you to this custom – it's enjoyable enough, despite an initial five-minute swoon…

HO GUOM AUDIO *Music*

☎ 824 3070; dnsonha@yahoo.com; 75 Pho Hang Bo; ☻ 8am-6pm Mon-Sat

The allure of Vietnamese pop music is generally lost on Western ears, but the more traditional music sold in this fine shop is downright soothing. Nothing evokes the sophisticated side of Vietnamese culture like exotic *dan bau, ca tru* or *ca hue* recordings (for more on these, see p131). Helpful staff will let you listen before buying.

KENLY SILK *Fashion*

☎ 826 7236; 108 Pho Hang Gai; ☻ 9am-8pm

Extravagant and colourful garments make for striking displays on three floors. Designs both light-hearted and chic are designed to sit daintily on shoulders and grab attention. Scarves, shoes, pyjamas, *ao dai* (Vietnamese national dress) and children's clothing (for apprentice fashion slaves) also are available.

KHAISILK *Fashion*

☎ 825 4237; www.khaisilk-boutique .com; 96 Pho Hang Gai; ☻ 9am-9pm

Some of Hanoi's highest-quality silk and linen garments are sold at this modern and well-lit shop. Fetching designs, mostly for women, elaborate upon traditional Vietnamese motifs, but also include jackets and robes thick enough to meet the needs of gals from less-balmy climes. Men will find a smattering of fairly conservative ties.

MAI GALLERY *Art*

☎ 828 5854; www.maigallery-vietnam .com; 183 Pho Hang Bong; ☻ 8am-8pm

One of Hanoi's leading purveyors of fine art, Mai Gallery is strikingly well lit, ensuring a careful inspection before you lay down your credit card. Many of the contemporary stalwarts are represented here, and gracious staff happily usher you from room to room. The handful of sketches by master To Ngoc Van are certainly worth a look.

🖼 THANG LONG GALLERY *Art*
☎ 825 0740; http://thanglongart
gallery.com; 41 Pho Hang Gai;
🕙 10am-8pm
This gallery has a lot of commercial art, like Bui Huu Hung's courtly
lacquers, but also exhibits a few of
Ly Tran Quynh Giang's brooding
blue oils.

🍴 EAT
🍴 BANH CUON GIA TRUYEN
Vietnamese $
☎ 280 108; 14 Pho Hang Ga;
🕙 8am-8pm
You might have to squeeze
your way into a chair during the
morning rush, but once you're
settled, your waitress will simply
put your food in front of you, no
questions asked. Delicate and
tasty *banh cuon* (silky steamed rice
crepes filled with minced pork,
mushrooms and ground shrimp),
served hot off the screen on which
they are steamed, is about all
they do here – and they do it with
expertise.

🍴 BUN CHA NEM RAN
Vietnamese $
20B Pho Ta Hien; 🕙 11am-3pm
The best food still comes from the
humblest of food stalls – and this
one's about as basic as they come.
It's a stools-on-the-pavement
affair run by a woman squatting
before an assemblage of little clay

barbecue grills. Order her delec-
table *bun cha* (rice vermicelli with
barbecued pork and vegetables)
and a plate of snappy *nem ran*
(spring rolls). It's the sort of food
that inspires repeated visits to
Hanoi.

🍴 CHA CA LA VONG
Vietnamese $
☎ 825 3929; 14 Pho Cha Ca; 🕙 10am-
2pm & 5.30-9pm
The antiquated atmosphere here
is legendary, and its rickety floors,
overcrowded tables and gruff wait
staff live up to the billing. Head
straight upstairs for the full-on
experience, and leave behind all
expectations of a relaxed midday

Help yourself at Cha Ca La Vong

 Le Cong Trinh
Cyclo driver

How old are you? I'm 59. **You look young for your age. Is that because you drive a cyclo?** Yes, I'm strong. **How long have you been driving a cyclo?** Thirty years. Since 1976. **What did you do before that?** I was in the army during the war. **Do you drive mostly tourists or locals?** Mostly tourists. **How many people can fit in your cyclo?** Two tourists. **How many Vietnamese people?** Five or six – two on the seat, one each on the arms of the seat, small children down in front, maybe one more up on the handle bars.

NEIGHBOURHOODS

OLD QUARTER

repast. It's a one-dish sweatshop, specialising in *cha ca* (fish grilled on your table with turmeric and dill, served with cold noodles and peanuts).

CHA CA THANH LONG
Vietnamese $

☎ 824 5115; 31 Pho Đ Thanh; ⏱ 10am-3pm & 5-10pm

Many locals habitually duck in here for a *cha ca* fix without the fuss of tourists shuffling in and out. The shambling atmosphere of Cha Ca La Vong (p48) is dispensed with, service is friendly and there's a bit more elbow room. It's a few blocks from its world-renowned predecessor.

GREEN TANGERINE
French $$$

☎ 825 1286; 48 Pho Hang Be; ⏱ 11am-11pm

The chaotic Old Quarter is not known for refined dining experiences, but Green Tangerine is the shining exception. It occupies a 1928 French townhouse sheltered behind a loggia and a front courtyard. It provides asylum for foreign gastronomes, with superb food, elegant presentation, a commendable wine list and fine service.

Get a taste of the French-colonial lifestyle at Green Tangerine

A FEAST OF SNAKES!

Le Mat, the 'snake village', is 6km from the Old Quarter. It is a grim little town where there's a snake on every plate, or at least part of one. Snake meat is prepared in a variety of ways – soups, steaks, however you like it. Ask a local about the taste and you'll get the usual 'tastes like *ga* (chicken)'. In some places, your server will show you your snake before it is slaughtered. They may even eviscerate it at your table and pour its blood into rice wine for you to drink. If you are the guest of honour, or the oldest male, you may be served a shot of rice wine with a still-beating snake heart. It makes you strong, they say.

Ask an environmentalist, and you'll be warned of the possibility that these snakes were captured in the wild. Indeed, many of the restaurants will tell you their snakes are wild, as that is what most Vietnamese customers want to hear. However, the vast majority of the snakes are farmed. Some of the restaurants in Le Mat advertise *thu rung* – forest animals – which, as a rule, are endangered in Vietnam. Avoid these places on principle.

Taxis can take you to Le Mat. It's over the Chuong Ðoung Bridge in the Gia Lam District.

Reserve for a romantic dinner, or drop by for a leisurely lunch.

🍴 HIGHWAY 4
Contemporary Vietnamese $$
☎ 926 0639; www.highway4.com; 5 Pho Hang Tre; ⏲ 8am-1am
Highway 4 is modern and stylish, and a Western influence is detectable in some dishes. But with crispy battered bee larvae and crocodile on the menu, it clearly beckons foreigners to meet the locals halfway. The catfish spring rolls with house mayo are an unexpected delight. The bar stocks the city's most palatable *ruou* (rice wines).

🍴 NHA HANG PHU MY
Vietnamese $
☎ 286 574; 45B Bat Dan; ⏲ 8am-7pm
It's tight quarters and flickering fluorescent lighting in this modest little joint, but the clientele is a happy bunch. Once you've ordered the house speciality you'll understand why. It's *pho xao bo*, which amounts to sautéed beef served on a plate of noodles with a thick, starchy gravy poured on top. The food is slopped onto your plate, but it packs lots of flavour.

🍴 PHO GIA TRUYEN
Pho $
49 Bat Dan; ⏲ 7-11am
The perfect broth for *pho* (rice-noodle soup) should look as though it was ladled from the river. It's opaque and brownish after beef bones have boiled in it for hours. Some places try to take the mystery out of *pho* by serving weak, see-through broths, but here you get the good stuff. Once you've experienced it you'll

NEIGHBOURHOODS

OLD QUARTER

understand why some can't start their day without a bowl of *pho*.

TAMARIND CAFÉ
Vegetarian $
☎ 926 0580; 80 Pho Ma May; ⏱ 6am-midnight
This cool and casual hang-out has the look and feel of a student coffee house. This being Hanoi, Tamarind attracts anyone dying for an omelette, but the varied vegetarian menu reflects an ambition to meld Asian culinary know-how and Western sensibilities. It's also a friendly spot for a pot of quality tea in the afternoon.

 DRINK

BIA HOI 68 HANG QUAT *Beer*
68 Pho Hang Quat; ⏱ 11am-10pm
Generally, *bia hoi* (draught beer) is a watered-down product sold cheaply. Here, they don't

---

BIA HOI BACK STORY

Put simply, *bia hoi* is 'fresh beer'. It is Pilsner brewed without preservatives. It lasts about a day and is priced accordingly – to ensure brisk sales. Interestingly, it was introduced to Vietnam by the Czechs, one-time allies during the Cold War. The exchange actually went two ways, and to this day many beers brewed in the Czech Republic contain hops imported from Vietnam.

---

water it down, and it's still damn reasonable (4500d a glass). The atmosphere is hard core, with tiny tables and parked motorbikes sharing a covered alleyway. For company you have cadres of old men who seem willing to exchange a toast. Have a few rounds, skip the food.

CAFE GIANG *Café*
7 Pho Hang Gai; ⏱ 8am-8pm
With bland chains taking over Hanoi's café scene, ancient holes such as this one have become revered treasures. To be sure, Cafe Giang's timeworn patina is almost a bleak exaggeration of communist-era non-chic. The front is wide open to frenetic Hang Gai, but within, amid chatty intellectuals congregating over strong drip coffees, it feels half a century away.

CAFE LAM *Café*
60 Pho Nguyen Huu Huan; ⏱ 7am-8pm
Lam is Hanoi's finest art-house café. It's a local institution, and over the decades it has accumulated an impressive collection of paintings left by talented patrons who couldn't afford to pay their tabs. The portrait of the man wearing a beret, above table No 7, takes the prize. Good coffee and pleasant company are big pluses.

French bohemia, Hanoi style, at Cafe Lam

☿ CAFE PHO CO *Café*
☎ 828 5080; 11 Pho Hang Gai;
⏲ 8am-9pm
Hidden sanctuaries are all over Hanoi, and finding them is a triumph, particularly when the setting is as rewarding as this one. There's no sign – look for the address and walk through the curio shop. Order your coffee at the secluded courtyard counter, carry it up several flights of stairs, and enjoy a show-stopping view of Hoan Kiem Lake.

☿ CAFE RUOU (WALKER'S PUB) *Bar*
2 Pho Yen Thai; ⏲ noon-10pm
The doorway to this little hideaway looks like the entry to an opium den, but inside is just a tidy little room in which to sample shots of *ruou* and other drinks. It's a nice place to stop by for a quick bracer.

☿ LEGENDS BEER *Microbrewery*
☎ 936 0345; www.legendsbeer.com.vn;
1 Pho Dinh Tien Hoang; ⏲ 9am-11pm
This is no *bia hoi* joint; rather, it's a microbrewery that produces decent lager, *dunkel* (dark beer) and *weizen* (wheat beer). It is in the homeliest building overlooking Hoan Kiem Lake, which qualifies as a fine excuse to grab a table on its 3rd-floor balcony – you get to look at the lake instead of the building.

You can also order from a decent menu.

▼ MAO'S RED LOUNGE *Bar*
☎ 926 3104; 7 Pho Ta Hien; ⏱ 4pm-late

With a relaxed vibe and unfussy décor, Mao's is a good spot to duck into for a few cold ones with friends. Its owner, Mr Mao, prefers to be addressed as 'the Chairman', and his refreshingly ironic attitude naturally adds to the atmosphere. Drop by Sunday night for a complimentary taste of Mao's hot-pot cooking.

▼ O QUAN CHUONG *Café*
☎ 213 5899; 24 Pho Hang Chieu; ⏱ 7am-9pm

Just down the street from the Old East Gate is this friendly spot for good coffee. It's a contemporary take on the classic Old Quarter coffee house. Western-scale tables and chairs make the foreigner feel welcome, but it's really a local hang-out.

▼ QUAN BIA MINH *Beer*
☎ 934 5323; 7A Dinh Liet; ⏱ 8am-midnight

This is a fun spot with a wrap-around balcony that affords good bird's-eye street-watching. Delightful people run Bia Minh, and their pet dog has the run of the place. The draft beer is a considerable notch above *bia hoi* standards, and the food is quite tasty.

▼ RED BEER *Microbrewery*
⏱ 826 0247; 97 Pho Ma May

Simple concept: the place is red and the homemade suds are fashioned after Belgian brews. It's popular with expats and tourists who've already had their fill of the street swill.

LEAD IN YOUR PENCIL

Ruou, the local rice wine, is not always fully appreciated by visitors, but among the Vietnamese it is considered a potent elixir. Its mystique has a lot to do with its supposed abilities to put a baguette in a man's pants, and draining a few shots in public is just about the surest way to establish camaraderie with the locals. Vietnamese women rarely indulge in the stuff, but there's no law prohibiting foreign women from giving it a whirl. In addition to the Viagra effect, it is also reputed to cure a thousand ills.

Many *ruou* bars showcase jars or vats infused with king cobras, scorpions, goat testicles, adult bears and other obscure organic matter. Indeed, the more dangerous and rare the creature, the more potent the drink is believed to be. If you must test the power of *ruou*, do the conscientious thing and stick with the herbal stuff. And don't overdo it, as the hangover is not very sexy. A good place for a *ruou* introduction is Highway 4 (p51 and p75), where the bar features an array of finely crafted bottles. Ask for 'zee-oh'. That's how it's pronounced.

PLAY

HO GUOM AUDIO
Traditional music

☎ 824 3070; dnsonha@yahoo.com; 75 Pho Hang Bo; admission free; ☷ 8pm Sun

A cool experience, not to be missed. On Sunday night, a slick little record shop is transformed into a comfortable cultural salon, with drapes covering the CD shelves and pillows and mats on the floor for guests to sit on. The attraction is traditional music, performed with theatrical flourishes by highly trained musicians in exotic attire. No synthesizers, drum machines or reverb. Complimentary tea and *ruou* are served.

JAZZ CLUB MINH *Jazz club*

☎ 828 7890; www.geocities.com /clb_nhacjazz; 31 Pho Luong Van Can; ☷ shows 9pm & 11.30pm

This is the grown-up, late-night side of Hanoi you probably never thought existed. Cool, mustachioed Quyen Van Minh is Hanoi's sax maestro – a cool cat who blows a mean horn. He holds court in his smoky jazz club nightly, often playing host to guest performers from around the world.

THANG LONG WATER PUPPET THEATRE *Theatre*

☎ 824 9494; www.thanglongwater puppet.org; 57B Pho Dinh Tien Hoang; admission 20,000-40,000d; ☷ shows 6.30pm & 8pm Mon-Sat, 9.30am, 6.30pm & 8pm Sun

You can't leave Hanoi without seeing a traditional water-puppet show. The shows, which appeal to all ages, are charming, picaresque entertainments accompanied by a traditional Vietnamese pit orchestra. Order your tickets early in the day for the best seats. Your hotel can probably help. See p25 for more on water puppets.

>HOAN KIEM LAKE & NHA THO AREA

Hoan Kiem Lake is central Hanoi's comely centrepiece, and its shaded paths invite an easy walk-around to admire the surrounding colonial cityscape. Amid such romantic tranquillity, a constant whir of motorbike traffic circles the lake's one-way boulevards, infusing the scene with modern energy. The lake is particularly lively during the early morning, when joggers, fast-walkers and rambunctious callisthenics brigades command its periphery. Late-rising tourists are drawn out by the lake's pavement cafés and an island-bound temple reached by footbridge.

Nearby, the blocks within the triangle formed by Pho Hang Bong and Pho Trang Thi house a fairly distinguished fashion district – its nucleus includes Pho Nha Tho and Pho Nha Chung, two compact corridors of boutiques and shops selling goods reflecting a contemporary Hanoi design aesthetic. Within the triangle, the curve of Pho Hang Hanh has established itself as Hanoi's lively backpacker nightlife zone. Good eats abound in hospitable brasseries and busy pavement stalls throughout the neighbourhood.

HOAN KIEM LAKE & NHA THO AREA

SEE

NGOC SON TEMPLE

admission 3000d; ⏲ **8am-5pm**
This island-temple, towards the northern end of Hoan Kiem Lake, is worth a detour – it can be reached via a picturesque footbridge. Inside, look for the preserved remains of a giant turtle, measuring 2.1m, that was captured in the lake (see the boxed text, below). The temple was founded in the 14th century, although its buildings date from the 18th century.

NHA THO (HANOI CATHEDRAL)

cnr Pho Nha Tho & Pho Nha Chung; donations accepted; ⏲ **5am-noon & 2-7pm**
Hanoi Cathedral's twin towers and Gothic arches elicit understandable comparisons with Paris' Notre Dame Cathedral. Nha Tho (also known as St Joseph's Cathedral) is smaller and greyer and in need of restoration, but, nevertheless, it cuts a striking figure. The interior is even more magnificent. Enter the grounds through the gate and look for the door on the left side of the church (Pho Nha Chung side).

SHOP

COCOON *Fashion & jewellery*

☎ **928 6922; cocoonvn@hotmail.com; 30 Pho Nha Chung;** ⏲ **10am-8pm**
The contemporary designs in this smart and charming little shop are quite striking. Silk garments for women are the mainstay, and these typically update traditional Vietnamese motifs. Many of the ensembles feature jazzed-up patterns and florid colours, and convey the fluid beauty of the *ao dai* (Vietnamese national dress) without the formality. Original jewellery is also sold here for very little money.

GOLDEN TURTLES

Turtles figure prominently in local lore. According to legend, 15th-century military hero Le Loi received a magic sword from a giant golden turtle in Hoan Kiem Lake. After defeating the Chinese and becoming Emperor Le Thai To, he returned the sword to the turtle. The lake owes its name, which translates as 'Lake of the Restored Sword', to this story. A monument, **Thap Rua** (Tortoise Tower), stands on a lump of soil near the lake's southern rim.

Giant turtles have appeared in Hoan Kiem Lake many times over the decades, and unconfirmed sightings are reported every year. Some sceptics say the turtles are planted for the sake of tradition. But of course, there are bound to be a few nay-sayers. The well-preserved specimen at Ngoc Son Temple (above) was found in 1968. It measures 2.1m and weighs 250kg.

Incidentally, young men in Hanoi are in the habit of referring to young women as 'turtles'. No doubt this is meant as a compliment.

HA GALLERY *Art*
☎ 928 7164; www.hagallery-vietnam.com; 18 Pho Hang Trong; ⏱ 9am-8pm
In this busy atelier, half a dozen painters crouch before easels and knock out reproductions of classic paintings such as the *Mona Lisa* and Edward Hopper's *Nighthawks*. The quality of the works varies and they would never be mistaken for the originals – but, let's face it, you can't afford the originals (these copies cost from US$40). You can also commission portraits of yourself, your sweetheart or your dog.

IPA-NIMA *Fashion accessories*
☎ 928 7616; www.ipa-nima-boutique.com; 17 Pho Nha Tho; ⏱ 10am-9.30pm
Designer Christina Yu, a native of Hong Kong, has gained an international following by creating stylish little handbags. Here you'll find all types, for all occasions: shoulder bags, tote bags, evening bags, summer bags and so on. Many project postmodern Asian chic, and all are darn cute.

L'IMAGE *Jewellery & décor*
☎ 928 6361; www.imagevn.com; 34 Pho Nha Chung; ⏱ 10am-8pm
This brightly lit shop gleams and glitters with the baubles displayed on its shelves. The jewellery is a celebration of beads and metalwork, much of it rather folksy and colourful. If nothing strikes your fancy, peruse the collection of impressive bronze teapots, copper buddhas, lacquered picture frames and other potential gift items.

MARENA *Décor*
☎ 828 5542; www.marenahanoi.com.vn; 28 Pho Nha Chung; ⏱ 8.30am-7.30pm
This tiny shop is packed with delicate handicrafts, all of them sophisticated and modern. Streamlined ceramic teapots and teacups, elegant wooden trays, chopsticks of lacquered wood, and boxes and bowls for all sorts of occasions are of original design and are smartly displayed. It won't take but a few minutes to assess the wares.

MOSAIQUE *Fashion & décor*
☎ 928 6181; mosaique@fpt.vn; 22 Pho Nha Tho; ⏱ 8.30am-8pm
You might easily walk right by this nondescript shop without peeking inside. But once you're in, you're likely to examine every piece of merchandise before leaving. The shelves feature a little of everything – silks, décor, homeware, jewellery – all in original designs and enticingly presented. You can also buy inexpensive silk-lined gift boxes.

Nguyen Kim Anh
Art repro dealer, Ha Gallery (p59)

Do you have a favourite artist or painting? Yes, Jack Vettriano. I love *The Singing Butler*, with the people dancing on the beach. **What types of paintings are most popular in your shop?** Paintings of Vietnamese girls. **There are a lot of Boteros – obese people dancing and playing cards and so on. Why so many of them?** They're funny. **Is this just a day job for the painters here? Do they also paint original works?** Our painters specialise in copying the masters. They have technique, but not ideas.

OLD PROPAGANDA POSTERS *Posters*

☎ 928 7943; 17 Pho Nha Chung; ⌚ 9am-8pm

The walls of this gallery are covered floor to ceiling with original pressings of propaganda art from the American War. The selection here is primarily of choice rarities (priced US$300 and up), and the inks are as vibrant as ever. They're all interesting to look at, whether conveying politically charged messages, or as optimistic bromides about farming. Many of the posters are strikingly beautiful.

ORIENTAL GALLERY *Art*

☎ 928 5747; 46 Pho Le Thai To; ⌚ 10am-9pm

Facing Hoan Kiem Lake, this gallery isn't as big as the Hang Gai establishments, and some of the works aren't as polished. Many of the artists are less well known, and some are perhaps more interested in taking chances than carving niches. These differences actually work in Oriental Gallery's favour. It's definitely worth a look.

PHUONG DONG ART SHOP *Décor*

☎ 829 1300; phuongdong45@yahoo.com; 1 Pho Ly Quoc Su; ⌚ 9am-8pm

The merchandise in this rustic shop is of the 'ersatz antique' variety, but the products are well made and very attractive. Much of the room is filled with pottery that appears ancient, and the shop's glass cases are loaded with *objets d'art* such as stone opium pipes that look as though they may actually work. You might find something for your mantelpiece.

SONG *Fashion*

☎ 928 8733; www.asiasongdesign.com; 27 Pho Nha Tho; ⌚ 9am-8pm

Valerie Gregori McKenzie's original designs have garnered her a strong following, and many travelling clothes hounds deliberately seek out her shop. McKenzie's company uses traditional Asian textile techniques, and avoids sweatshop environs by contracting with independent Vietnamese women, who do much of the actual stitchwork. The clothing is casual, comfortable and stylish, generally using subtle, earthy colour schemes.

SUFFUSIVE ART GALLERY *Art*

☎ 828 8359; www.suffusiveart.com; 2B Ngo Bao Khanh; ⌚ 10am-9pm

This is a smallish gallery, rather than a mind-boggling multilevel emporium, so the handful of artists represented here are shown in the best possible light. The gallery clearly favours contemporary expression, and the art generally pushes the envelope, often in ways that jar with the traditional Asian fondness for serene natural scenes.

EAT

⊮ BANH GHOI
Vietnamese $

52 Pho Ly Quoc Su; ⏱ **10am-7pm**
A *banh ghoi* is like a meat patty filled with pork, glassy noodles, mushroom and seasonings. A plate of three served piping hot in this fine little place is a tasty treat on a cold day. Tourists are starting to eat here, but clearly the friendly woman who runs the joint values her regular patrons, and standards remain as high as ever.

⊮ FANNY
Ice cream $

☎ **828 5656; 48 Pho Le Thai To;** ⏱ **10am-9pm**
Facing the lake and resembling a *belle époque* creamery, Fanny's is the place to be on a summer's eve. French-style ice cream and crepes are served with an artistic flourish, looking like tropical drinks. Fanny especially excels with the unusual flavours of ginger, cinnamon and coconut. Fresh tropical-fruit ice creams are seasonal.

⊮ I-BOX
European & contemporary Vietnamese $$$

☎ **828 8820; 32 Pho Le Thai To;** ⏱ **8am-midnight**

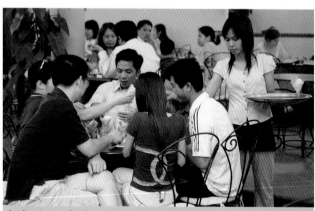
Stop for an ice-cream fix at Fanny during your evening stroll around the lake

Tapas in Hanoi? You'll find it at La Salsa

The lush décor here is an assemblage of cheetah-skin patterns, overly large couches and extravagant colours. The atmosphere becomes even more interesting when the local nouveau riche file through the doors and the bartenders rattle their cocktail shakers with flair. It's over the top, but the food and service are very good, and most nights the place features live music, movies or slick DJs.

🍴 LA SALSA
European tapas $$
☎ 828 9052; 25 Pho Nha Tho;
🕙 10.30am-midnight
This appealing tapas joint, with its soothing and cheery bar room, is popular with foreigners. No doubt they're drawn to its relaxed vibe and elegant comfort, the amiable staff and the exceptional food. Delicate pork ribs and perfectly fried calamari are mouthwatering, and you can also order steaks, lamb cutlets and other things that go well with potatoes.

DRINK
🍸 CAFE NHAN *Café*
☎ 826 9861; 39D Ngo Hang Hanh;
🕙 8am-10pm
Nhan is right in the armpit of the curving Hang Hanh backpacker ghetto, which, if you've come this way, is exactly where you want

Kick-start your day at Hapro Coffee Kiosk beside Hoan Kiem Lake

to be. It has a fine vantage point of the street, and it looks and feels like a spin-off of Rick's, from *Casablanca*. It's a lively place for a cup of coffee.

▼ FUNKY MONKEY *Bar*
☎ 928 6113; 15B Pho Hang Hanh; ⏰ noon-2am
The Monkey's moodily lit tables have an undeniable allure – in fact, they're very flattering, making this a cool bar in which to admire your friends. The bar staff can shake a wide variety of cocktails, from tried-and-true classics to modern exotic experiments. Occasionally, DJs spin some of the best beats around.

▼ HAPRO COFFEE KIOSK *Café*
Pho Le Thai To; ⏰ 7am-9pm
There's no topping Hapro's location, beneath the flowering flame trees a few skips from Hoan Kiem Lake. You'll want to order something just for the excuse to sit down. The menu is voluminous, but stick with the espresso drinks, artsy fruit beverages, light sandwiches and breakfast fare and you'll be happy.

▼ MOCA *Café*
☎ 825 6334; 14 Pho Nha Tho; ⏰ 7am-10pm
If the local drip coffee doesn't float your boat, head here to find the type of coffee you're used to.

Moca roasts its own beans, and regulation-size tables and chairs are up to foreign standards – no squatting required. The atmosphere ain't at all bad, especially when staff stoke up a fire in winter.

PLAY

☆ HO GUOM XANH *Floorshows*
☎ 828 8806; 32 Pho Le Thai To; admission free; ⏱ shows 9pm

No place better represents the slick, contemporary side of Hanoi's nightlife. The cheerily uniformed bar staff peddle steeply priced bottles of Johnny Walker Black with the persistence of used-car salesmen, and the wildly gyrating go-go dancers are a throwback to Paris revues – naughty, but not X-rated. When the singers come out, however, it's plain that Hanoians are as sentimental as ever.

☆ NEW CENTURY *Disco*
☎ 928 5285; 10 Pho Trang Thi; admission free; ⏱ 9pm-2am

Young Hanoians pack into this huge dance hall and shake it up to loud techno and hip-hop-influenced beats. The place draws an adoring crowd when popular singers from HCMC take the stage. DJs are accompanied by shimmying go-go dancers. A multitude of bars afford space to enjoy a relaxed drink or sing karaoke.

>FRENCH QUARTER & HAI BA TRUNG DISTRICT

Much of the appeal of Hanoi's French Quarter is in its colonial architecture. The tree-lined boulevards have a grand feel to them, and they are all the more interesting for the modern Hanoi life that now predominates along the pavements. As in the Old Quarter, each street has its share of ad hoc food stalls and clusters of *xe om* (motorbike taxi) drivers, but here the pavements are actually wide enough to accommodate them.

The French took control of Hanoi in 1882, and created a new district for bureaucrats and traders. With its gorgeous Opera House, fine government buildings and lovely villas, the French Quarter still exudes Parisian style. Pho Trang Tien, the main axis, is lined with art galleries and bookshops, and worthwhile museums are distributed throughout the neighbourhood.

Travellers spending time in the French Quarter will doubtless feel the pull of Lenin Park and the excellent restaurants of the Hai Ba Trung District.

FRENCH QUARTER & HAI BA TRUNG DISTRICT

◉ SEE
Ambassadors' Pagoda (Chua Quan Su) 1	B3
Cho 19-12 (19 December Market).......................... 2	C3
History Museum.................. 3	F3
Hoa Lo Prison ('Hanoi Hilton')................ 4	B3
Lenin Park Main Gate...... 5	B5
Metropole Hotel................ 6	E3
Museum of the Vietnamese Revolution . 7	E3
Museum of Vietnamese Women.......................... 8	C3

⬢ SHOP
Dong Phong Art Gallery . 9	D3
Infostones Bookshop ... 10	D3
Ipa-Nima 11	E5
Life Photo Gallery 12	D3
Mai's Cafe 13	D5
Nguyen Frères 14	E3

🍴 EAT
Au Lac House 15	E4
Bo Tung Xeo................. 16	C6
Cafe 129...................... 17	C6
Chim Sao 18	D6
Club 51 19	E2
Com Chay Nang Tam ... 20	B4
Emperor....................... 21	E4
Hai San Van Anh 22	D6
Highway 4 23	C6
Hoa Sua School............ 24	B4
Le Beaulieu................. (see 6)
Le Tonkin 25	C4
Metropole Hotel........... (see 6)
Nam Phuong 26	E4

Opera Club.................... 27	E3
Pho 24........................... 28	D3
Pho Thin 29	D5
Quan An Ngon 30	A2
Restaurant Bobby Chinn 31	D3

🍸 DRINK
Au Lac Cafe 32	E3
Club 51 .... (see 19)
Lan Chin 33	E3
Le Club .... (see 6)

★ PLAY
Central Circus 34	A5
Hanoi Cinematheque ... 35	D3
Hanoi Opera House 36	E3
Mosaique Livingroom ... 37	C4

Please see over for map

SEE

AMBASSADORS' PAGODA (CHUA QUAN SU)

☎ 825 2427; 73 Quan Su; donations accepted; ⏲ 9am-5pm

HQ for the Vietnam Buddhist Association, Quan Su is one of the city's busiest houses of prayer. It's especially active on the first and 15th days of the lunar month, when even casual Buddhists come to make an offering. On your way in buy some incense from a pavement vendor, then light them and poke them into the courtyard urns – it's good luck!

CHO 19-12 (19 DECEMBER MARKET)

Pho Ly Thuong Kiet; ⏲ 8am-9pm

Supermarkets and malls are sprouting up all over town as many Hanoians adopt the shopping habits of Western consumers. However, Cho 19-12, found between Pho Hoa Lo and Pho Quang

HAUNTED MARKET

Cho 19-12 market (above) is named for the date of a 1946 battle fought here between Vietnamese insurgents and French troops. Initially, after the market opened in the late 1970s, it was known as 'Hell's Market' because many locals recalled that casualties from the battle were buried on the spot. Whether the story is true or not remains a mystery.

Trung, is an old-style market geared towards some of Hanoi's more traditional residents. It's worth a walk-through, particularly during the busier morning hours. By noon, it's a surreal picture of a carnival that's past its peak.

HISTORY MUSEUM

☎ 825 3518; 1 Pho Trang Tien; admission 15,000d; ⏲ 8-11.30am & 1.30-4.30pm Tue-Sun

A beautiful French-colonial building and engrossing exhibits make for a winning combo. Archaeological artefacts fill up most of the ground floor, while upstairs concentrates on recorded history up to 1945 (the Museum of the Vietnamese Revolution, p71, takes it up from there). The life-sized diorama depicting Vietnamese cave-dwellers is tops, but the scale-model battle scenes are also hard to walk away from.

HOA LO PRISON ('HANOI HILTON')

cnr Pho Hoa Lo & Pho Hi Ba Trung; admission 5000d; ⏲ 8-11.30am & 1.30-4.30pm Tue-Sun

US POWs ironically dubbed Hoa Lo the 'Hanoi Hilton' during their stay here (Senator John McCain was among them), but Hoa Lo's history is much deeper. The French built it to detain Vietnamese dissidents, and the exhibits manage to emphasise the horrid conditions

under French rule while simultaneously painting a somewhat rosy picture of POW life here. Nonetheless, it's well worth a visit.

🎥 METROPOLE HOTEL
☎ 826 6919; 15 Pho Ngo Quyen

The 1953 Citroën parked in front of Hanoi's legendary Metropole says it all, for behind the hotel's wedding-cake exterior you'd never know the French got their rumps kicked at Dien Bien Phu (in 1954). When it opened in 1901, this was one of the classiest hotels in all of Asia. It still oozes colonial extravagance. Take a look around, and have an exotic cocktail at the Bamboo Bar.

LENIN PARK: THE ODD & THE BEAUTIFUL

Lenin Park's foreboding main gate on Pho Tran Nhan Tong doesn't project an inviting aura to the outside world, but ignore the natural impulse to move on – pay the 2000d admission charge and have a look around. The park is a peaceful refuge within the hectic city, and it's also more than a little strange.

We'll forgo a logical geographic approach to the park and instead lure you in with the peaceful part. The centrepiece, amid carefully groomed gardens, is dark, placid Bay Mau Lake. Getting around it requires a brisk walk or jog, which is what you'll see most people doing in the early morning or late afternoon. This being a Vietnamese lake, live waterfowl are vastly outnumbered by paddle boats that resemble giant plastic geese.

But we're not yet finished with the peaceful part. The lake loops around a section of park called Orchid Island, where gardeners tend to a jaw-dropping variety of orchids that, unfortunately, are not labelled. Stroll the little paved paths and cross the bridge and you're sure to encounter love birds quietly holding onto each other the way love birds do in this country. Throughout the park, open spaces are generally taken by badminton players and people kicking shuttlecocks fashioned from shredded rice sacks weighted by metal washers. A narrow-gauge railroad runs a loop round the lake, and rickety carnival rides painted with cartoony animals beckon all children. Patio cafés offer a legitimate excuse to just sit down and watch.

Things get a little weird along the north side of the lake, where an entertainment called 'water ball' is inexplicably popular. The water ball is an inflatable sphere that one or two people can crawl into. They zip it up and fill it with air and shove you off onto the water, where you can roll around like a hamster until the air runs out. This pastime seems dangerous and vaguely humiliating, and yet you can't be blamed for wanting to try it out. A little way to the north of the hamster ride is Lang An Toan Safety Village, a miniature car track where children can learn to appreciate traffic safety. It's sponsored by Ford and New York Life Insurance, two companies obviously looking forward to the day when Hanoi's motorbikes disappear and the city turns into one giant traffic jam (in which no-one ever crashes their SUV).

Lenin Park's main gate is on Pho Tran Nhan Tong, near the corner of Đ Le Duan, in Hai Ba Trung District.

History Museum (p67): admire it inside and out

MUSEUM OF THE VIETNAMESE REVOLUTION

☎ 825 4151; 216 Đ Tran Quang Khai; admission 10,000d; ⏱ 8-11.45am & 1.30-4.15pm Tue-Sun

This one's a little intense, but relevant, for even as communist economics fade there's no taking away the fact that this small, impoverished nation earned its independence. Photos, documents, yellowed newspapers and unsigned oils tell the story. A guide might be able to explain some of the more puzzling artefacts – the taxidermied pig, for instance.

MUSEUM OF VIETNAMESE WOMEN

☎ 825 9938; 36 Pho Ly Thuong Kiet; admission 10,000d; ⏱ 8am-4pm Tue-Sun

The Vietnamese women celebrated here are graceful, wily and strong as all hell. Among the fuzzy photos usually displayed in Hanoi museums are some fascinating artefacts, including homemade machetes, a knife with an explicit caption noting it slashed at an oppressor's neck, and the ragtag garments worn by a female spy who pretended to be crazy. The top floor showcases beautiful textiles made by ethnic-minority women.

WORTH THE TRIP: PERFUME PAGODA

A visit to the dramatic Perfume Pagoda requires a full day. The trip gets you out into the countryside for a boat ride and a hike up to a hilltop complex of pagodas and shrines, some hanging from cliffs, others set inside caves. It's Vietnam's biggest pilgrimage site, especially during the second and third lunar months. It can be quite festive and chaotic during these times and on weekends year-round.

The one-hour boat ride is a doozy. Local women, exhibiting inexhaustible strength, row boats that may be carrying a dozen or so Westerners. You move steadily up a sinewy stream between beautiful limestone cliffs. The ensuing two-hour hike up to the pagodas can be strenuous, but there are numerous rest stops along the way. There are even sleeping stations, but these are mostly for frail old ladies making the pilgrimage. Be prepared with good shoes, as it can slippery.

Though a religious site, the Perfume Pagoda has a strong commercial side to it, which adds to its excitement even if it detracts from the site's spiritual power. A hike up can evoke scenes from Fellini's *La Dolce Vita*. In this case, the pestering paparazzi have turned into hawkers selling postcards, books and cheap curios. It's part and parcel of the experience.

The Perfume Pagoda is 60km southwest of Hanoi. You'll need to hire a car and driver to get to the river, then hire a boat woman to row you up the stream. Your hotel front desk can help arrange the car. Touts will lead you to the boats.

SHOP

DONG PHONG ART GALLERY *Art*

☎ 936 0481; www.dongphonggallery.com; 14 Pho Ngo Quyen; ⏰ 10am-8pm
One of Hanoi's best art galleries, this neat shop stands out by selecting a small number of works by serious artists. Owner Pho Hong Long has a discerning eye, is very easy-going, and speaks English well enough to teach you about the current scene. Older works by beaux-arts alumni are also exhibited here. Mr Pho can arrange studio visits with some artists.

INFOSTONES BOOKSHOP *Books*

☎ 826 2993; 41 Pho Trang Tien; ⏰ 10am-9pm
There are several bookstores along Pho Trang Tien, and most have a few things for English-speaking readers to flip through. This shop is worth checking out for its solid selection of large-format, four-colour books on art, design and architecture.

IPA-NIMA *Fashion accessories*

☎ 933 4000; www.ipa-nima.com; 34 Pho Han Thuyen; ⏰ 10am-9.30pm
This is a branch of a popular local chain (see p59) that sells clothing by designer Christina Yu.

📷 LIFE PHOTO GALLERY *Art*
☎ 936 3886; 39 Pho Trang Tien;
🕐 9am-9pm

Finely printed enlargements of Do Anh Tuan's documentary photography cover the walls of this small shop. Do has been capturing reflective and provocative images, mostly in black and white, since 1971. A 5x7-inch print (US$12) makes a nice gift or keepsake.

📷 MAI'S CAFE *Coffee*
☎ 622 7751; 96 Pho Le Van Huu;
🕐 10am-7pm

Vietnamese drip coffee is an acquired taste, and it can be somewhat addictive. You can keep your habit going for a few weeks after returning home if you buy fresh beans or grounds from this fine-smelling establishment. It ain't all that cheap, but if you're still reading, you're probably hard core.

📷 NGUYEN FRÈRES
Décor, silks & antiques
☎ 933 1699; www.nguyenfreres.com;
5 Pho Hai Ba Trung; 🕐 9am-8pm

Finely selected antiques, quality reproductions and stylish silks are attractively displayed in this beautiful two-storey shop, which projects a sophisticated and appealing hybrid of Asian and European aesthetics. Cool Deco lamps, groovy print scarves, old buddhas, French Catholic statuettes and H'mong textiles are just some of the items sold here. The shopkeepers will offer you hot tea, to induce you to linger awhile.

🍴 EAT

🍴 AU LAC HOUSE
Contemporary Vietnamese $$
☎ 933 3533; aulachouse@ftp.vn; 13 Pho Tran Hung Dao; 🕐 8am-11pm

On a sultry evening, you'll want to be seated on the terrace of Au Lac House, sipping cocktails and dining on finely prepared Vietnamese dishes. It's housed in a roomy colonial villa and the service is attentive and efficient, but the food is not to be outshined. The kitchen deftly concocts rustic country dishes and more-exotic innovations.

🍴 BO TUNG XEO
Vietnamese $
☎ 821 7809; 47 Pho Mai Hac De;
🕐 noon-9pm

It's undeniably cool having dinner on a covered rooftop along happening Pho Mai Hac De. Bo Tung Xeo requires some work to find (walk through the downstairs *pho* restaurant and up the stairs at the back), which naturally adds to its appeal. The speciality is a marinated sliced beef dish, which you and your friends grill at your table. Along with cold beer it makes a hearty repast.

NEIGHBOURHOODS

FRENCH QUARTER & HAI BA TRUNG DISTRICT

🍴 CAFE 129
Western breakfast $

☎ 821 6342; 129 Pho Mai Hac De;
🕑 7.30am-10pm

Five sisters and their mother operate this neat little eatery that's
known city-wide for its satisfying
omelettes, pancakes and fresh
fruit juices. They get it right, too.
Naturally, the place attracts a lot
of foreigners hankering for something other than *pho* in the early
hours, but local students often
claim several tables as well.

🍴 CHIM SAO
Contemporary Vietnamese $

☎ 976 0633; www.chimsao.com; 65 Ngo
Hue; 🕑 11.30am-2pm & 6pm-midnight

One of Hanoi's smartest dining
options, with subtly creative food
and an arty, Asian-boho atmosphere. It gets busy on weekend
evenings, when foreigners have
the run of the place. It's especially
nice for lunch.

🍴 CLUB 51
Asian & European $$$

☎ 936 3069; club51lythaitho@ftp.vn; 51
Pho Ly Thai To; 🕑 10am-11pm

The grand, open floorplan of this
villa sets the tone for a special
evening out. Huge Chinese lan-
terns cast a warm glow over the
upstairs dining room, and an array
of couches and tables, dispersed
among potted plants, creates

Dine in comfort and style at Club 51

Hanoi's most luxurious space. The menu ranges from East to West without indulging in the fusion concept.

🍴 COM CHAY NANG TAM
Vegetarian Vietnamese $

☎ 942 4140; 79A Pho Tran Hung Dao; ⏱ 10am-2pm & 5-9.30pm

Hidden down a crooked pedestrian alley, Nang Tam is isolated, quiet and elegant. The tasty and traditional vegetarian cuisine comprises mostly simulated-meat dishes that stand up on their own merit. It's popular with expat vegetarians and practising Buddhists, who line up for tables on the first and 15th days of the lunar calendar. The good sample menus offer a varied introduction.

🍴 EMPEROR
Contemporary Vietnamese $$$

☎ 826 8801; emperor@ftp.vn; 18 Pho Le Thanh Tong; ⏱ 11.30am-2pm & 5.30-10.30pm

For festive and exotic atmosphere it doesn't get any better. Thankfully, Emperor follows through with sophisticated and rewarding contemporary Vietnamese food. Choose your setting: the lush courtyard, inside the traditional Asian wooden house, or up on the balcony. Be sure to include an order of shrimp paste on sugar cane, which makes for a fun and delicious starter.

The lush courtyard of the Emperor restaurant

🍴 HAI SAN VAN ANH
Vietnamese seafood $$

19 Pho To Hien Than; ⏱ noon-10pm

This unassuming spot has been known to overcharge foreigners, though the excellent seafood is still very reasonable by non-Hanoi standards. The gripe may be that the atmosphere is still very much of the Hanoi street variety. If you can live with that, round up some friends and order huge platters of fried squid and some of the city's best French fries.

🍴 HIGHWAY 4
Contemporary Vietnamese $$

☎ 976 2647; www.highway4.com; 54 Pho Mai Hac De; ⏱ 8am-1am

This is a newer branch of the deservedly popular Old Quarter restaurant (see p51). There are a lot of other interesting restaurants and cafés nearby, and if you're staying in the French Quarter you'll probably want to swing by for a *ruou* (rice wine) or a good meal. It attracts Vietnamese and foreigners in equal numbers.

🍴 LE BEAULIEU
French $$$$

☎ 826 6919; sofitelhanoi@hn.vnn.vn; 15 Pho Ngo Quyen; ⌚ 6.30-10.30am, noon-2pm & 6.30-11pm

In the Metropole Hotel (p70), Le Beaulieu serves exquisite French cuisine in a refined atmosphere. It has been operating since 1901. The kitchen crew, schooled under Chef Didier Corlou's watch, delivers an expertly prepared *coq au vin*, and competent servers quietly ensure a smooth and romantic dining experience. Sunday brunch is also very popular. Reservations are always recommended.

🍴 LE TONKIN
Vietnamese $$

☎ 943 3457; 14 Ngo Van So; ⌚ 11am-2pm & 6-10pm

The neocolonial dining experience is toned down at Le Tonkin. Its appeal is in the quiet, simple elegance of its setting, in a backstreet villa. You can take your leisure in the homy dining room or in the courtyard among leafy banana trees. Excellent food draws inspiration from the street and the country, and the cooks here don't meddle much with tradition.

🍴 NAM PHUONG
Vietnamese $$

☎ 824 0926; 19 Pho Phan Chu Trinh; ⌚ 11am-2pm & 5-10pm

For upscale Vietnamese in a large and beautiful villa, you can't go wrong with this place. While the kitchen does a commendable job with many regional dishes, the menu particularly shines with seafood specialities like soft-shell crab in tamarind sauce. An acoustic ensemble plays traditional music nightly, often working in some Western numbers for novelty's sake.

🍴 OPERA CLUB
European & Vietnamese $$

☎ 933 3740; operaclub.hn.vn@gmail.com; 5 Dang Thai Than; ⌚ 7am-11.30pm

This lively supper club draws a mixed crowd of ascending locals and foreigners. Breakfast, lunch and dinner are served here, but the place comes alive at night, when live music (Viet cabaret, jazz, flamenco) gets cooking. Seating on several levels is arranged around an open stage. The kitchen favours quality ingredients, including beef and lamb from down under. Music starts at 9pm.

START COOKING

Learning to cook Vietnamese cuisine is an excellent way to familiarise yourself with the local culture. Several cooking courses in Hanoi include an instructive shopping excursion to a local market, and hands-on preparation of the city's culinary delights followed by a great lunch. The following courses last about four hours.

Highway 4 (☎ 715 0577; 54 Pho Mai Hac De; US$32) See p75 for more about this restaurant.

Hoa Sua School (☎ 942 4448; 28A Pho Ha Hoi; US$30)

Metropole Hotel (☎ 826 6919; 15 Pho Ngo Quyen; US$50) See p70 for more about this hotel.

🍴 PHO 24
Pho $

☎ 936 5259; 1 Hang Khay; ⏱ 8am-10pm

Pho 24 is a chain from Saigon, which you might not think would do well in Hanoi, where *pho* (rice-noodle soup) originated. But think again. Locals dig the Pho 24 style. The soup is a fairly light and quick meal served with a plate of fresh greens, in accordance with the southern custom. The dining room, decorated in a modern streamlined style, is spotlessly clean.

🍴 PHO THIN
Pho $

13 Pho Lo Duc; ⏱ 8-10.30am

You'll get a very good bowl of *pho* in this family-run joint. Just be prepared for a down-home *pho*-eating experience: order yours on your way in, elbow your way into a seat, and kick aside the little piles of tissues at your feet. Within seconds, the aromatic steam rising from your bowl will remind you why you came.

🍴 QUAN AN NGON
Vietnamese $

☎ 942 8162; 18 Phan Boi Chau; ⏱ 6am-10pm

As hygiene becomes a growing concern, many middle-class Hanoians have begun to shun traditional street vendors. This place addresses the problem by placing impeccably clean food stalls in the lush courtyard of a restored villa. All signs indicate that well-to-do Hanoians love the concept, and many dress up for a meal here. It's a very upbeat and fun place. Before sitting down to your menu, walk around and see what looks good in the stalls.

🍴 RESTAURANT BOBBY CHINN
International $$$

☎ 934 8577; www.bobbychinn.com; 1 Pho Ba Trieu; ⏱ 11am-late

This is one of Hanoi's most celebrated contemporary establishments. Its chef is a New Zealand native who trained in Paris, with a sensibility that's cosmopolitan to the extreme. The décor and menu are modern and playful, and the spirit carries over to the magnificent and artistically presented food. Bold strokes and seasonal ingredients are Chef Chinn's stock in trade.

DRINK

☎ AU LAC CAFE *Café*
☎ 825 7807; 57 Pho Ly Thai To; ☾ 7am-10pm
Au Lac's shaded front patio is a pleasant spot for an afternoon coffee. You've got a French villa behind you and, to keep you in touch with modern Hanoi, you've got the blur of traffic whizzing before you. You can also order a light bite or the mixed drink of your choosing.

☎ CLUB 51 *Lounge*
☎ 936 3069; club51lythaitho@ftp.vn; 51 Pho Ly Thai To; ☾ 10am-11pm
The downstairs lounge at Club 51 (also a restaurant; see p74) is a live-music venue where acoustic ensembles and some of Vietnam's best cabaret singers perform to an adoring crowd. You can also get a mean martini here.

☎ LAN CHIN *Beer*
2 Pho Trang Tien; ☾ 11am-11pm
This pavement beer hall has dozens of tables lined up beneath a corrugated tin arcade. It's just

outside the Museum of the Vietnamese Revolution. The draughts are decidedly superior to the swill sold on Bia Hoi Corner (p18), and you can also get pretty decent food – hot pots, fried fish dishes and such. If you're travelling with friends and you like beer, you'll have a raucous time here.

☎ LE CLUB *Bar-café*
☎ 826 6919, ext 8212; 15 Pho Ngo Quyen; ☾ 3pm-late
With its twirling ceiling fans and 'Champagne bar' billing, Le Club, in the Metropole Hotel, harks back to the leisurely French period, as does its signature drink, the ruby-hued Graham Greene Martini. (Greene stayed at the hotel and doubtless drank at this bar.) Le Club's appeal broadens significantly at tea time (3pm to 5.30pm), when it offers its irresistibly decadent chocolate buffet.

CAFÉ STREET
Pho Trieu Viet Vuong (C6), in the Hai Ba Trung District, has two blocks lined with café after café, many of them quite inviting. Cafe Mimosa, at No 127, with birdcages hung from trees over pavement tables, and Cafe 55, at No 55 towards the quiet end of the strip, are particularly attractive. The street hops in the morning and evening, when Hanoians (mostly men) enjoy nursing small coffees for hours.

Hoang Vinh Nam
Traditional doctor

Why is ruou (rice wine) so popular in Hanoi? Mostly people think it's good for sex. They say, 'the husband drink, the wife enjoy'. **How widespread is the practice of infusing ruou with endangered animal parts?** All over Asia. Even some medical doctors believe in it. Peasants, highly educated people – doesn't matter, they drink it. **In your opinion is there any validity in this belief?** No. Definitely none at all. **Does it even taste good to drink rice liquor with, say, the penis of a tiger soaked in it?** No. And that's not just my opinion. Even people who drink it don't enjoy the taste. **Can you recommend an environmentally friendly alternative?** You mean Viagra?

Luong Hai Hoa
Coffee and tea vendor

How long have you been doing business here? More than 20 years. My mother sold tea here before me. **Do you have to pay rent for this spot?** I own this spot. **You must know the neighbourhood well.** Yes. I have sold coffee here for many years. I know people. They walk down the street, stop and have tea or coffee. **The job has its pluses?** Before I worked in an office, but I'm old now. I like doing this. It's near my room. I make OK money. **Do you plan to keep doing this a long time?** I don't know. Maybe 20 years more. After me, I don't know. Maybe no-one will sell tea here. **Things are changing?** Yes. Now I make more money parking motorbikes. Used to just be coffee, tea and snacks.

PLAY

CENTRAL CIRCUS *Circus*

Lenin Park; admission 50,000d, for Sun morning show 20,000d; ☽ **shows 8pm Wed-Sun, 9am Sun**

The huge permanent tent at the northern end of Lenin Park is home to Hanoi's Central Circus. The Russians introduced circus arts during their era of influence here, and the Vietnamese have retained a fondness for it. The Sunday morning show is geared towards children.

HANOI CINEMATEQUE *Cinema*

☎ **936 2648; 22A Pho Hai Ba Trung; 1-night membership 10,000d (negotiable)**

Congrats if you find this spot, hidden deep down a pedestrian path off Pho Hai Ba Trung. It's an art-house cinema that screens nondubbed foreign films. Before the film, have a drink or a light bite in the convivial courtyard café –

it's a gathering spot for expats and visiting film-lovers.

HANOI OPERA HOUSE *Opera*

☎ **565 1806; www.ticketvn.com; Pho Trang Tien**

With fewer than 1000 seats, there's really not a bad seat in Hanoi's legendary Opera House. If a show is on, take advantage, because it is a magnificent space and makes for a grand evening out. Performances occur irregularly and vary fairly widely, with classical music being common.

MOSAIQUE LIVINGROOM *Nightclub*

☎ **822 6458; 23 Ngo Van So**

This intimate nightspot books touring artists from around the world. Expats appreciate the Livingroom because it caters to Western preferences, so if you're hankering for a taste of home, head here – the vibe can be very positive. It's a private club that opens its doors to the public fairly often.

SINGING BIG

The Hanoi Opera House (above) is highly treasured as an architectural gem and as a historic site. The French built it in 1911, having modelled it on Paris' Palais Garnier. They were understandably pleased with their work, and in the 1990s the French government contributed to its restoration.

The building has long been cherished by the communist government of Vietnam as well. On 16 August 1945, a committee of citizens stood on its balcony and announced that the Viet Minh had taken control of the city.

The theatre's Vietnamese name, Nha Hat Lon, translates as 'House Sing Big'.

>BA DINH

A considerable tract of land in the heart of the Ba Dinh district is devoted to the memory of Ho Chi Minh, and the diminutive Ho himself lies peacefully at the centre of it all in his Soviet-style mausoleum. After paying your respects, make a morning of it by visiting the Ho Chi Minh Museum and Ho's stilt house, both well worth quick tours. Even better is the tightly assembled Viet Nam Military History Museum, which depicts the determined effort involved in forging Vietnamese independence.

If you're really breezing, stroll by the district's lovely old villas on your way down to the Temple of Literature, just a few blocks away in Dong Da. You'll need to catch a ride out to visit the excellent Vietnam Museum of Ethnology, in Ba Dinh's outer extremity, but it's worth the journey.

BA DINH

◎ SEE
Flag Tower 1 D3
Ho Chi Minh Mausoleum . 2 C2
Ho Chi Minh Museum 3 C3

Ho Chi Minh's Stilt
House 4 B2
Presidential Palace 5 C2
Viet Nam Military
History Museum 6 D3

⅋⅋ EAT
Brothers Café 7 D4
Seasons of Hanoi 8 D1

👁 SEE

👁 HO CHI MINH MAUSOLEUM

cnr Đ Houng Vuong & Le Hong Phong; admission free; ⏱ 8-11am Tue-Thu, Sat & Sun Dec-Sep, last entry 10.15am

The mausoleum building is an un-inviting grey hulk overlooking an asphalt parade ground, but within it lies Ho Chi Minh's embalmed body, and that's what hundreds of visitors come to see each day. Show up early to ensure you make it through the line before the mausoleum's early closing time. Cameras and bags must be left at a counter before you enter. See also p10.

👁 HO CHI MINH MUSEUM

☎ 846 3752; Pho Ngoc Ha; admission 5000d; ⏱ 8-11am & 1.30-4.30pm Tue-Thu, Sat & Sun

This is a fascinating, although sometimes obscure, museum. The concept seems to be to convey Ho's ideology in an ethereal manner through exhibits that are artistic, at times impressionistic, and always philosophical and thought-provoking. Naturally, it's not for raving anticommunists. English-speaking guides are available and recommended, unless you just want to do a quick walk-through (which is still worthwhile).

A DYING WISH DENIED

The immense Ho Chi Minh Mausoleum was built from 1973 to 1975. Within it lies the late Vietnamese leader, em-balmed, and surrounded by military guards. Each day a procession of admir-ers files past for a quick glimpse. To be sure, seeing Uncle Ho in the flesh is a goose-pimple-inducing experience. All of this fuss, however, defies the humble leader's stated desire to be cremated and have his ashes scattered through-out Vietnam – although the mausoleum does contain materials gathered from around the country.

👁 HO CHI MINH'S STILT HOUSE

☎ 804 4529; 1 Bach Thao; combined stilt house & palace grounds 10,000d; ⏱ 8-11am & 2-4pm, closed Mon & Fri afternoon

Uncle Ho's humble stilt house, hidden behind the far grander Presidential Palace, is a stylised peasant home. He supposedly lived here from 1958 until his death in 1969. It's an interesting image – the kindly old leader liv-ing the simple life, amid gardens and koi ponds, while American B-52s groaned overhead. Check out the helmet next to the bank of telephones.

👁 PRESIDENTIAL PALACE

☎ 804 4529; 1 Bach Thao; combined palace grounds & stilt house 10,000d; ⏱ 8-11am & 2-4pm, closed Mon & Fri afternoon

Guards still watch over Uncle Ho's humble stilt house

Admission to Ho's house also gets you onto the grounds of the Presidential Palace, which was home to the governor general of French Indochina. It was built in 1906. It isn't open to the public, but pause to admire it from outside – it's quite a contrast to Ho's two-bedroom abode.

🅒 VIET NAM MILITARY HISTORY MUSEUM

☎ 823 4264; www.btlsqsvn.org.vn in Vietnamese; 28A Pho Dien Bien Phu; admission 10,000d; ⏲ 8-11.30am & 1-4.30pm Tue-Sun

Vietnamese military history is not a conventional matter of tanks and battalions, which is why this museum is so engrossing. Exhibits include ample evidence of Vietnamese resourcefulness: bamboo spikes, crudely tinkered firearms, buffalo horns, crazy-looking torpedoes. Quality photos get you behind Viet Minh lines. Outside the building, an artistic heap of B-52 wreckage is worth a walk-around, and be sure to go to the top of the Flag Tower.

NEIGHBOURHOODS

BA DINH

Bahnar communal house, Museum of Ethnology

 VIETNAM MUSEUM OF ETHNOLOGY

☎ 756 2193; Nguyen Van Huyen; admission 10,000d; ☼ 8.30am-5.30pm Tue-Sun

A taxi ride out to this museum, several kilometres west of the Ho Chi Minh Mausoleum, is highly recommended for anyone interested in the Vietnamese hill tribes who have maintained traditional lifestyles despite wars and globalisation. Indoor exhibits focus on arts, textiles and celebrations, but these could be better presented. Far superior is the outdoor compound of traditional structures, through which you are free to wander. The huge Bahnar communal house is stunning.

🍴 EAT

🍴 BROTHERS CAFÉ

Vietnamese $

☎ 733 3866; 26 Pho Nguyen Thai Hoc; ☼ 11.30am-2pm & 6.30-10pm

VO NGUYEN GIAP

Hanoi's most illustrious living hero, General Vo Nguyen Giap, was still kicking as of this writing. (He was born around 1912, putting him in his mid-90s.) General Vo joined Ho Chi Minh during WWII, when he helped organise Viet Minh forces to resist the Japanese occupation of Vietnam. He then led the lengthy and ultimately successful campaign against the French, culminating with his decisive victory at Dien Bien Phu. During the American War he served as commander-in-chief of the People's Army of Vietnam. For the better part of two decades, the North Vietnamese battled the South Vietnamese Army and the Americans, until the US finally withdrew its troops in 1973. It was a costly victory (about one million Vietnamese died in the fighting) for which General Vo is still largely celebrated in Vietnam. He lives in a French villa near the Ho Chi Minh Mausoleum.

CONSIDERING SAPA

If you're in Vietnam for just a few days, you can forget about working Sapa (10 hours by train from Hanoi) into your plans. This mountain market town, where H'mong and Dzao people hawk their wares, requires a journey of at least three days. If that's workable for you, a trip to this scenic and culturally fascinating region is sure to be rewarding.

There are a variety of tours that include Sapa and the surrounding villages. These usually include treks. Handspan (p111) offers sensitive hiking and biking tours of the region. **Topas Travel** (☎ 715 1005; www.topas-adventure-vietnam.com; 52 To Ngoc Van, Hanoi) operates an eco-lodge 18km from Sapa and provides guided treks throughout the region.

Independent travel is not difficult. Book a sleeper on an overnight train from Hanoi through the **Hanoi train station** (☎ 825 3949; 120 Đ Le Duan; ⏱ 7.30-11am & 1.30-4pm); tickets are around 200,000d. Hotels abound in Sapa. **Victoria Sapa Resort** (☎ 020-871 522; www.victoriahotels-asia.com; d from US$126) offers luxuriant accommodation and private transport from Hanoi aboard its 'Victoria Express' train.

In the shaded courtyard of a restored 250-year-old Buddhist temple, Brothers offers a peaceful atmosphere and friendly service. The setup is very casual, with an all-you-can-eat buffet and salad bar. The selection is huge, with Vietnamese standards reflecting Western influence here and there. It's often busy with locals and foreigners.

🍴 SEASONS OF HANOI
Vietnamese $$
☎ **843 5444; 95B Pho Quan Thanh;**
⏱ **11.30am-2pm & 6-11pm**
Though tour groups flood the joint from time to time, Seasons of Hanoi offers exquisite French-colonial atmosphere and fine Vietnamese cuisine. The papaya salad is a good start, and grilled beef with lemon grass and chilli is a standout main. Before or after your meal, enjoy a drink in the mahogany bar.

>DONG DA

Dong Da, just west of the French Quarter, isn't a part of town in which visitors spend a lot of time, but few skip it altogether. The main carrot here is the Temple of Literature, Hanoi's ancient scholarly refuge. The excellent Vietnam Fine Arts Museum is just across the street, and you can easily divide a highly cultural morning between these two venerable institutions. Or split them up with a midday massage and a relaxed lunch at KOTO. Van Mieu is a shopping and dining strip that appears to be steadily fleshing out. All are within a few blocks' radius. Spend part of a day roaming these concentrated streets and you'll be a real gone Dong Da daddy.

DONG DA

◉ SEE
Temple of Literature (Van
Mieu) 1 B3
Vietnam Fine Arts
Museum 2 C2

🛍 SHOP
Coco Silk 3 C3
Craftlink ....(see 3)

🍴 EAT
Cafe Smile 4 C3
KOTO 5 B3

▼ DRINK
Cafe des Artes ....(see 7)
Cafe Lam 6 C3

✦ PLAY
Maison des Artes............7 C3

BA DINH

P Doi Can

Le Hong Png

Đ Hung Vuong

P Dien Bien Phu

P Hoang Dieu

P Nguyen Tri Phuong

Hanoi Citadel
(Military
Area)

Giang Vo

Đ Tran Phu

P Nguyen Thai Hoc

Chu Van An

Khuc Hao

Cao Ba Quat

2

**OLD
QUARTER**

Van Mieu

4

Nguyen Khuyen

P Cat Linh

Quoc Tu Giam

1

3
7

DONG DA

Quoc Tu Giam

6

Nam Ngu

Hanoi (Ga
Hang Co)

Đ Le Duan

N Van Huong

Tran
Quy Cap

P Tran
Hung Dao

P Ton Duc Thang

Thien Hung

P Yet Kieu

Đ La
Thanh

P Kham Thien

Đ Nguyen
Luong Bang

Ngo Cho Kham Thien

**FRENCH
QUARTER**

Xa Dan

To Apocalypse
Now (1km)

0   400 m
0   0.2 miles

NEIGHBOURHOODS

DONG DA

 SEE

TEMPLE OF LITERATURE (VAN MIEU)

☎ 845 2917; Quoc Tu Giam; admission 5000d; ⊙ 8am-5pm

Founded in 1070, the Temple of Literature is a compound of traditional buildings, interior courtyards and tranquil gardens. It is interesting for both its architecture and its history, and you can easily lose track of time wandering the grounds, snapping photos and watching traditional musicians perform. Show up soon after the gates open to beat the tour buses.

VIETNAM FINE ARTS MUSEUM

☎ 733 2131; www.vnfineartsmuseum .org.vn; 66 Pho Nguyen Thai Hoc; admission 20,000d; ⊙ 9am-5pm Tue-Sun

This is Hanoi's best museum, and it's enormous, so set aside a couple of hours to appreciate the works. Highlights are the extraordinary wood carvings from the 14th century; wartime paintings (many of which are humanistic rather than propagandistic); and the collection of ethnic costumes that surpasses the display at the Vietnam Museum of Ethnology (p86). There's also a pleasant café and a decent gift shop. See also p12.

GRADUATING WITH HONOURS

The Temple of Literature (Van Mieu) was founded in 1070 by Emperor Ly Thanh Tong, who dedicated it to Confucius in order to honour scholars and men of literary accomplishment. Vietnam's first university was established here in 1076 to educate the sons of mandarins. In the Garden of the Stelae, flanking a beautiful square pond, 82 stone turtles bear huge stelae on their backs. These stone slabs are inscribed with the well-worn names of students who received doctorates at the university from 1442 to 1778.

 SHOP

COCO SILK Fashion

☎ 747 1535; cocosilk@hn.vnn.vn; 37A Van Mieu; ⊙ 8.30am-7pm

This is a high-end shop that sells silk garments for women and men. Contemporary looks are teased out of traditional Vietnamese styles. You can also shop for embroidered curtains, handbags and shoes.

CRAFTLINK Ethnic crafts

☎ 843 7710; www.craftlink-vietnam .com; 43 Van Mieu; ⊙ 9am-6pm

The wares sold in this large shop are produced in Vietnam's ethnic villages, and the profits are reinvested in those communities. (Goods sold elsewhere in Hanoi are sometimes copies produced

Spend a morning soaking up the culture and history of the Temple of Literature

NEIGHBOURHOODS

DONG DA

in local sweatshops, cutting in on the ethnic crafts trade.) Clothing, textile goods, shoes, ceramics and art are available here.

EAT

🍴 CAFE SMILE
International $$

☎ 843 8850; 5 Van Mieu; 🕒 7am-9pm
Here's a cheery place. Like the better-known KOTO (right), Smile trains and employs former street kids. They're doing a fine job of it, making tasty pizzas, sandwiches and Vietnamese standards. Walk through the kitchen and head

upstairs to the stylish, well-lit and quiet dining rooms.

KOTO
Vietnamese $

☎ 747 0337; www.koto.com.au; 59 Van Mieu; 🕒 7am-3pm daily, 6-9pm Fri-Sun
KOTO is a well-loved nonprofit that trains and employs disadvantaged youth. (The name is an acronym of 'know one, teach one'.) It is also a damn fine spot for a quick bite or a more involved meal. It has a café, a dining room and two bars, including a 'treetop terrace' overlooking the Temple of Literature.

Help out disadvantaged kids while helping yourself to a meal at KOTO

DRINK
CAFE DES ARTES *Café*
☎ 747 3435; 31A Van Mieu;
🕙 9am-4pm
On a rooftop terrace overlooking
the Temple of Literature, Cafe des
Artes' Francophone owner has
created a literary atmosphere.
It's a literary salon of sorts, with a
library, European espresso drinks
and fine teas from Vietnam and
China. Out the back, an appealing
wooden house sits on the roof,
providing a traditional environment for drinking tea.

CAFE LAM *Café*
56 Quoc Tu Giam; 🕙 7.15am-11pm
Around the corner from the Temple
of Literature is one of Hanoi's most
unassuming cafés, with space for
two tables inside and enough
pavement for two more out front.
The little café is sometimes singled
out by expats for its fine street-
watching vantage point. There are
others like it, sure, but not so near
the Temple of Literature.

 # PLAY
APOCALYPSE NOW *Disco*
☎ 971 2783; Star Bowl Centre, Pham
Ngoc Thach; 🕙 8pm-1am
Hanoi's best-known nightclub
is an after-dark crossover zone
where Hanoians, tourists, expats,
straights and gays congregate.
The scene here can be very
interesting. Some complain about
the presence of prostitutes, while
others simply shrug them off.
If you're up for dancing, this is
your best bet. Tunes range from
techno to soulful oldies. It rocks on
weekends.

MAISON DES ARTES
Beauty salon
☎ 747 3435; 31A Van Mieu; massage
US$10-20; 🕙 9am-4pm
The professional masseuses in this
soothing salon will knead every
muscle on your body for a very
reasonable sum. You can also have
your nails filed or your hair cut, or
get a facial.

>WEST LAKE & TRUC BACH AREA

A few blocks north of the Old Quarter, Ho Tay (West Lake) is the largest of Hanoi's numerous lakes. The area along the lake's eastern shore is slowly being developed as a wealthy enclave, with contemporary-style villas and modern high-rise hotels that have already sparked the emergence of restaurants and shops. More charming is Truc Bach Lake, a small lagoon that was cut off from West Lake centuries ago. At its heart is the unexpectedly quiet Ngu Xa island, a secluded realm that's great for walking. Truc Bach is rimmed by inviting cafés and restaurants that fling open their doors to catch lake breezes in the warmer months. The busy blocks between the lakes and the Old Quarter are home to an excellent gallery exhibiting contemporary art, and to a museum-like shop dealing in antiques sourced from Vietnam's hill-tribe communities.

WEST LAKE & TRUC BACH AREA

◉ SEE
Quan Thanh Temple 1 C4
Tran Quoc Pagoda 2 C3

⌂ SHOP
54 Traditions Gallery 3 D4
Art Vietnam 4 D4

ⵏ EAT
Bun Cha 5 D4
Dragon Boat 6 C3
Food Shop 45 .... 7 C3
ILU Lounge 8 C3
Kitchen 9 B1
Vine Wine Boutique
Bar & Cafe 10 B1

▼ DRINK
Highlands Coffee 11 C3

★ PLAY
Paddleboats 12 C3
Zen Spa 13 B1

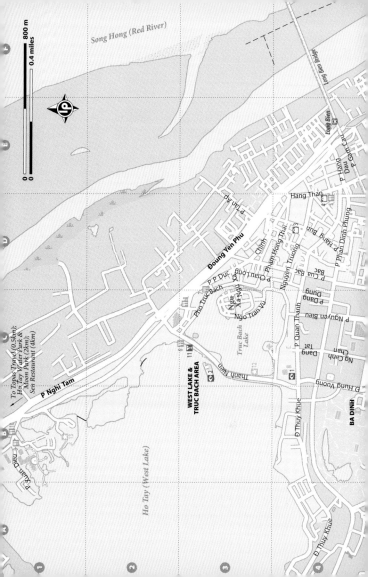

SEE

⊙ QUAN THANH TEMPLE
Pho Quan Thanh; admission 2000d;
⏱ **5am-7pm**
This temple has a lovely setting, removed from the street by a spacious courtyard. The real attraction here is the 4000kg statue of Huyen Thien Tran Vo, whose giant toenails have been polished by adoring hands for centuries. The statue is lacquered bronze, made in 1677. The temple is on the shore of Truc Bach Lake.

⊙ TRAN QUOC PAGODA
Thanh Nien; admission 5000d;
⏱ **5am-7pm**
On the eastern shore of West Lake, this is one of the oldest pagodas in Vietnam. The current structures are very impressive and date back to 1842. The pagoda is just off the road that divides West Lake and Truc Bach Lake.

 # SHOP

⊡ 54 TRADITIONS GALLERY
Art & antiques
☎ **715 0194; www.54traditions.com; 30 Pho Hang Bun;** ⏱ **10am-6pm**
This shop has a mind-boggling collection of antiques from Vietnam's hill-tribe communities. All of it's for sale, but it's worth taking an informed tour of the three floors,

Impressive Tran Quoc Pagoda

especially if co-owner Nguyen Thi Nhung is on hand. She's one of Hanoi's most knowledgeable curators of ethnic crafts, and she will patiently explain any item that strikes your fancy. All purchases are documented for export.

⊡ ART VIETNAM *Art*
☎ **927 2349; www.artvietnamgallery .com; 30 Hang Than;** ⏱ **10am-5pm**
One of Hanoi's most reputable galleries, Art Vietnam is an essential stop for any serious collector. Works by local (and some foreign) artists address contemporary issues of rapidly changing Hanoi.

Hoan Thi Minh Hong
First Vietnamese person to visit Antarctica (1996)

How did you end up going to Antarctica? It was the 50th anniversary of Unesco, and they invited young people from a few countries to go on an expedition. They chose Vietnam to be one of the countries, and a contest was held. I applied for it, I wrote an essay, and they chose me. **Why do you suppose no Vietnamese person had ever gone there before you?** There was no opportunity. Travelling there is hella expensive. **What did you think of the place?** The scenery is spectacular. It's mysterious. It feels good to go to a place that doesn't belong to any country. **Now that you have broken the ice, so to speak, do you envision waves of Vietnamese tourists flocking down to Antarctica?** Vietnamese are not adventurous, and most think Antarctica's on the North Pole. To them it sounds like hell. Too cold.

Look for Nguyen The Son's power-line cityscapes, Nguyen Manh Hung's studies of Hanoi traffic and Peter Steinhauer's awesome large-format photographic prints.

EAT

BUN CHA
Vietnamese $

34 Hang Than; ⌚ **10am-3pm**
Next to Art Vietnam gallery is this fine little mother-and-daughter operation. They do one thing only (*bun cha* – a dish of rice vermicelli with barbecued pork and vegetables), and they do it well. Work it into your plans if you're visiting the gallery.

DRAGON BOAT
Vietnamese seafood $$

☎ **829 4894; Tay Long 3, Thanh Nien;** ⌚ **10am-9pm**

PHO CUON AXIS
The street stalls along Ngo Tran Vu are all the excuse you need to plan an early-evening stroll around Ngu Xa (C3), the island community within Truc Bach Lake. The stalls here specialise in a dish called *pho cuon* – marinated beef strips and herbs wrapped in a soft 'rice crepe'. It's delicious and light, perfect on a warm evening. Hanoians seem to regard it as appealing date food, and many couples converge on Ngu Xa whenever they get a yen for the stuff.

It can be quite a hoot having dinner aboard a boat painted to look like a dragon as it tools around West Lake. The menu emphasises seafood but generally covers the Vietnamese staples, including novel snake and pigeon platters. Vegetarians will have much to choose from. If you're travelling with a group, you can charter the entire boat for 600,000d.

FOOD SHOP 45
Indian $

☎ **716 2959; 59 Truc Bach;** ⌚ **10am-11pm**
The front of this popular family-run restaurant is thrown wide open so that diners can fully appreciate Truc Bach Lake. It's a lively spot that lures in expats with a fine selection of Indian curries, kebabs, tandoori grills and Indian breads. To top it off, the staff is friendly and the décor's stylish.

ILU LOUNGE
Contemporary Vietnamese $$

☎ **715 0656, ext 36; 18 Đ Yen Phu;** ⌚ **8am-midnight**
On the 8th and 9th floors of the ILU office tower, this cool, contemporary space offers an upward escape from the hustling city below. However, panoramic windows and a rooftop terrace ensure Hanoi doesn't get completely blotted out. Vietnamese and pan-Asian dishes are prepared nicely,

as are lunchtime tapas plates. It's perfectly reasonable to come here for drinks and the view.

⊞ KITCHEN
Sandwiches $

☎ 719 2679; http://kitchen.so-9.com; 9 Xuan Dieu; ⏲ 7am-9pm

In the shadow of the Sheraton, cute little Kitchen offers healthy non-Vietnamese sandwiches. Homesick expats love it, and if you can relate to their cravings for PB&J or a burrito, then you're likely to gravitate here. Everything's fresh and made with care.

⊞ SEN RESTAURANT
Vietnamese $$

☎ 719 9242; 10 Lane 431, Đ Au Co; ⏲ 11am-2pm & 6-10pm

Sen looks like a stylised temple, with doors wide open to catch a breeze off West Lake. Regional Vietnamese, traditional-market-inspired dishes are prepared in speciality stalls. The buffet concept works well in this setting, giving you the opportunity to sample as many dishes as you want. Sen makes an excellent introduction to Vietnamese cuisine.

⊞ VINE WINE BOUTIQUE BAR & CAFE
International $$$

☎ 719 8000; www.vine-group.com; 1A Xuan Dieu; ⏲ 9am-11pm

Vine is widely considered to be one of Hanoi's finest restaurants. It certainly has the city's most comprehensive wine cellar. Gourmet pizzas are a headliner, but the menu also includes excellent steaks, burgers, clay pots and a smattering of Thai dishes. It may sound over-ambitious, but the kitchen manages to keep all balls in the air. Hybrid East-West décor creates a contemporary atmosphere.

DRINK

⊠ HIGHLANDS COFFEE *Café*

☎ 829 2140; 34 Thanh Nien; ⏲ 7am-9pm

Aboard a big old ferry boat, Highlands gets you out on the water without actually setting sail. Its decks offer a fine vantage point and a chance to catch a refreshing breeze while enjoying smoothies, shakes and ice cream. You can also order a light meal or breakfast. The signature product, of course, is coffee.

PLAY

⭐ HO TAY WATER PARK & MOON PARK *Water park*

☎ 753 2757; adult/child 50,000/30,000đ; ⏲ 9am-9pm Wed-Mon 15 Apr-Nov

On summer's most sweltering days it may seem like all of Hanoi

NEIGHBOURHOODS

WEST LAKE & TRUC BACH AREA

Join the love birds flocking to ride a paddleboat across the lake

converges on this water park, 5km north of the city centre. After cooling off on the water slides and in the refreshing pools, you can catch a stiff breeze on a double-corkscrew roller coaster in the adjacent Moon Park.

⭐ PADDLEBOATS *Paddleboats*

Thanh Nien; per boat 20,000-25,000d
From the boat launches along Thanh Nien you can sail out onto Truc Bach or West Lake in your own private plastic goose. It's a paddleboat, actually, so you'll have to do some work to get it moving. Locally, riding a giant goose is considered romantic, so bring along your honey-pie and paddle to bliss.

⭐ ZEN SPA *Spa*

☎ 719 9889; www.zenspa.com; Đ Yen Phu; ⏰ 9am-7.30pm
Traditional Asian massages and herbal therapies are provided in an admirably soothing environment of smartly crafted wood huts amid lush gardens. It's near the Sheraton.

>HALONG BAY

Traditional trading boats in Halong Bay

>HALONG BAY

Few visitors to Hanoi can resist the opportunity of seeing Halong Bay, which is just a few hours east of the city. It's a special place where nature hits you over the head with its beauty.

It doesn't require a naturalist's sensitivity or an artist's honed eye to appreciate Halong's harmonious design, the way land and sea conspire to fill the horizon with extraordinary shapes and colours. From the deck of a slowly moving boat, compositions of limestone islands and jade-hued waters continually evolve before your eyes.

Hundreds of islands dot the bay, most of them tall hillocks jutting straight out of the water, topped by trees, brush and bird life. Small sandy beaches ring some of the islands, while within other islands hollowed-out caves dazzle the traveller with cathedral-like stalactites. The largest island, Cat Ba, has a densely forested national park, a beach resort, and remote villages in which visitors can arrange a homestay.

It is possible to do a quick day trip on Halong Bay, but the bay is best appreciated on an overnight cruise that allows time for swimming, kayaking, beaching and visiting caves and floating fishing villages hidden amid the bay's 366 islands. The greatest concentration of islands is some 50km from the docks of Haiphong and Halong City, and they are best appreciated aboard a slow-moving boat. Staying a night on board may well be a once-in-a-lifetime experience.

Many tours include a night in Cat Ba Town, often with a second night aboard a boat. If you have just one night, sleep on board. The only compelling reason to opt for a Cat Ba hotel is if you are prone to seasickness or want to get an early start for Cat Ba National Park. No matter how you choose to go about it, all is very easily arranged from home or through the numerous tour agencies in Hanoi.

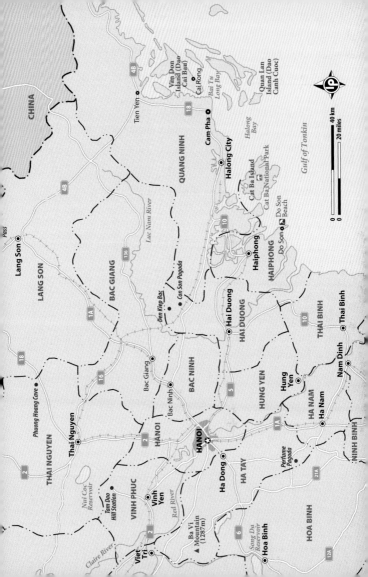

HALONG BAY
CAT BA ISLAND

Halong Bay's largest island has a varied topography of abruptly ascending peaks, narrow valleys, sandy beaches, tropical evergreen forests, swampy bottomlands and secluded villages. A network of trails can lead a curious and physically fit traveller into the heart of this complex natural environment.

Cat Ba Town (p107) has its pluses and minuses, but even if it's not exactly your cup of tea, it can make an excellent base for exploring both Cat Ba National Park (p108) and the nearby islands and beaches. One of Cat Ba's selling points is that it's easy to access independently, freeing you from packed shuttles and tour boats. The island can be reached quickly from Haiphong or Halong City via hydrofoil.

The best weather on Cat Ba Island is from late September to November, when the temperature is mild and the skies are mostly clear. It cools off from December to February, but can still be quite pleasant. The rainy season lasts from February to April, and the summer (June to September) is often hot and humid.

INFORMATION

The **Tourism Information & Development Office** (☎ 031-368 8215; ⏰ 7am-9pm) is on the waterfront drag, next door to the Tra My Hotel. Staff can help arrange village homestays, motorbike rental (US$4/5 per half/full day) and tickets for the hydrofoil.

Most hotel front desks can help arrange transport to Cat Ba National Park, as well as guides, boat trips into the bay and boat taxis out to the beaches and floating seafood restaurants.

Half of Phuong Phuong Restaurant, on Cat Ba Town's waterfront, has given way to rows of computer terminals for internet access. Around the corner, on Đ Nui Ngoc, Internet Explorer also has plenty of terminals. Rates at these places seem to be at the discretion of whoever's minding the store, but are likely to start at around 2000d.

Many hotels will help with currency exchange if you're carrying US dollars. Ask at the front desk. Internet Explorer also changes money.

FESTIVALS & EVENTS

Mark 1 April on your calendar, even if you're not interested in a career change, for one of Cat Ba's biggest public celebrations takes place on this day. Although Traditional Fishing Career Day has a clearly stated pro-fishing theme,

HALONG BAY

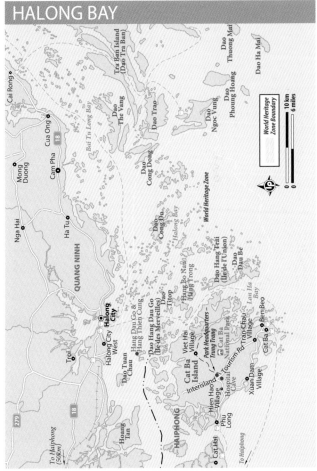

Cai Rong

Cua Ong

18

Cam Pha

Mong Duong

Nga Hai

Ha Tu

QUANG NINH

Tra Ban Island
(Dao Tra Ban)

Dao Thuong Mat

Dao Ha Mai

Dao The Vang

Dao Tra

Bai Tu Long Bay

Dao Phuong Hoang

Dao Ngoc Vung

Dao Cong Dong

World Heritage Zone

Halong Bay

Dao Cong Do

World Heritage
Zone Boundary

10 km

6 miles

0

0

Halong City

Halong City West

Dao Tuan Chau

Hang Dau Go &
Hang Thien Cung

Dao Hang Dau Go
(Iles des Merveilles)

Dao Titop

Hang Bo Nau
Hang Trong

Dao Hang Trai
(Ile de l'Union)

Dao Dau Be

Lan Ha Bay

Viet Hai Village

Cat Ba Island

Park Headquarters –
Trung Trang

Cat Ba
National Park

Ben Beo

Tran Chau Village

Cat Ba

Toi

Hospital
Tourism Rd
Cave

Xuan Dam Village

HAIPHONG

Hien Hao
Village

Interisland

Phu Long

Hoang Tan

18

279

*To Haiphong
(50km)*

Cat Hai

To Haiphong

the date actually commemorates a visit by Ho Chi Minh in 1959. The purpose of his visit was to promote the liberation movement. Essentially, Uncle Ho was fishing for support. Nowadays, edible, non-ideological seafood is the order of the day.

GETTING THERE & AROUND

The fastest way to reach the island is by hydrofoil (100,000d), which departs Haiphong several times daily and, at latest report, once daily from Halong City. The trip from Haiphong or Halong is 45 minutes by hydrofoil. You'll need to make your way to these embarkation points by train from Hanoi, a trip that generally takes around 2½ hours (see p141 for details). Tour companies such as Open Tour Sinh Café (p111) can assemble the entire transport ticket package for you. Book at

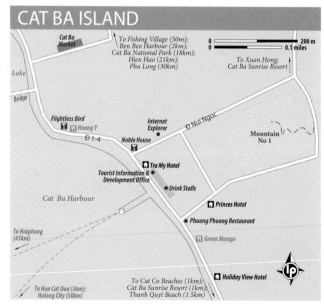

CAT BA ISLAND

Cat Ba Market

To Fishing Village (50m);
Ben Beo Harbour (2km);
Cat Ba National Park (18km);
Hien Hao (21km);
Phu Long (30km)

0   200 m
0   0.1 miles

To Xuan Hong;
Cat Ba Sunrise Resort

Lake

Bridge

Flightless Bird
Hoang Y

Internet Explorer

Đ Nui Ngoc

Mountain No 1

Đ 1-4

Noble House

Tra My Hotel

Tourist Information & Development Office

Drink Stalls

Cat Ba Harbour

Princes Hotel

Phuong Phuong Restaurant

Green Mango

To Haiphong (45km)

To Hon Cat Dua (3km);
Halong City (50km)

To Cat Co Beaches (1km);
Cat Ba Sunrise Resort (1km);
Thanh Quyt Beach (1.5km)

Holiday View Hotel

least a day ahead, and show up early. The boats are often fully booked and tend to depart as soon as they're full.

You'll be able to walk around Cat Ba Town, but a motorbike gives you greater flexibility in terms of beaches and exploring the park. You can hire a *xe om* (motorbike taxi) for a few hours (price is negotiable), but it's more economical to rent your own motorbike from the Tourism Information & Development Office (see p104). Riding a motorbike in Vietnam can be tricky business for the beginner, but Cat Ba is a relatively sane place in which to dip your feet in the stream.

For a few dollars you can also hire boat taxis, some of which are charmingly rustic, from the wharf in central Cat Ba Town. These can get you to floating restaurants and to other islands, where uncrowded beaches await. Hotel front desks can help.

 SEE
CAT BA TOWN
Rapidly transforming into a tourist resort, Cat Ba Town is more convenient than picturesque. However, it's not altogether lacking in charm. The town is clearly divided between its bayfront hotel zone, with newly paved roads and modern buildings, and the older,

more roughshod fishing villa... where the locals live. The fishi... village is worth a stroll, as is the local market, and you can usually hire someone to row you out through the harbour and over to the nearby beaches, giving you an up-close look at the local seafaring lifestyle. The tourist zone is generally overrun with backpackers and vendors selling imitation pearls.

At its best, Cat Ba can be rowdy and fun, but during the cold and wet months it can feel like an underattended carnival – all flashing lights and not enough life. Take a stroll along the waterfront during the early morning, when the harbour is busy with departing fishing boats.

BEACHES
The biggest, most easily reachable beaches are **Cat Co 1**, **2** and **3**, and **Thanh Quyt**, all a little more than 1km south of Cat Ba Town. Each of these beaches is nestled within its own protected cove. You can walk or take a *xe om* to the Cat Co beaches by following the waterfront road, Đ 1-4, south of town. Thanh Quyt is a little further afield via hilly Đ Ngoc.

The beaches near town can be crowded on weekends, but you can easily get off on your own by hiring a boat taxi to one of the small islands nearby. Your hotel should be able to help arrange this.

CAT BA NATIONAL PARK

If you have the time and the gumption, Cat Ba National Park can be very rewarding. The most accessible periphery of this national park is far from pristine, and getting into the wilder heart for which the park is treasured will require at least a full day's commitment – as well as some serious physical effort. The park, measuring some 150 sq km, is home to some unique and rare plant and animal species, most notably the golden-headed langur (see the boxed text, opposite) – if you spot one in the park, consider yourself very lucky.

Many Halong boat tours include a stop at Cat Ba National Park for a short but strenuous midday hike. Typically, you'll walk up a steep trail to the top of **Ngu Lam Peak** (225m). On the peak, hikers can admire a panoramic view from a rickety watchtower that once was used by the North Vietnamese Army to spot enemy planes. On windy days, climbing the watchtower can be a terrifying experience, after which you'll appreciate your life and loved ones much more than you did before.

If you are not doing a tour you can see much more of the park by hiring a guide who can take you there on a motorbike during the quieter early-morning hours. This is actually a much better way to experience the park, as the crowds

Treading carefully through a cathedral-like cave interior

DECLINE OF THE LANGURS

The golden-headed langur monkey (also known as the François monkey) is unique to Cat Ba Island and a few smaller islands nearby, but the species is on the verge of disappearing. It's estimated that during the 1970s and '80s some 500 to 800 langurs were killed or captured by poachers. After the founding of Cat Ba National Park in 1986, poaching fell dramatically, but the estimated loss of around 100 monkeys in the 1990s nevertheless was nearly catastrophic. It is believed there are now only around 60 langurs left.

have your own a torch (flashlight) to see anything.

For avid hikers, there is a challenging 18km (six to 10 hours) hike through the park's karsts and freshwater swamp forests. The hike ascends several steep mountain summits and ends at remote **Viet Hai village** (below). You'll need to hire a guide who knows the hike. This is most easily arranged through the front desk of your hotel in Cat Ba Town. If it has been raining the trail can become extremely slippery, even dangerous. Consult with your guide and other locals to determine whether the hike is worth undertaking.

can, at times, be nonexistent and your options are far greater. The earlier you hit the trails, the better your chances of spotting deer, hedgehogs and monkeys. Birds, of which some 70 species have been sighted, are apt to appear any time of day. The park, which includes both marine and terrestrial components, also attracts migrating waterfowl, which feed and roost on the beaches in the mangrove forests.

Within the park, two caves are open to visitors and are worth visiting. **Hospital Cave** oozes historical significance, as it served as a secret, bomb-proof hospital during the American War. **Trung Trang Cave**, just south of the park entrance along the main drag, is more easily accessible, though you'll want to

PARK HEADQUARTERS

Trung Trang is the most useful headquarters in the park. It is accessible via the Interisland Tourism Rd, which links up with the main road north of Cat Ba Town. It is a 30-minute ride by minibus (10,000d), which you can catch at hotels in Cat Ba Town (prearrange a pick-up, and tickets, at your hotel's front desk). You can also hire a motorbike in town (20,000d).

VIET HAI VILLAGE

This remote village, in the heart of Cat Ba National Park, is a small ethnic enclave in an idyllic setting. The villagers here maintain a very traditional lifestyle, growing rice and raising pigs and chickens, although the local economy is somewhat bolstered by tourism. Some of the villagers inhabit humble thatched huts constructed of mud, straw and wooden posts. For a truly unforgettable experience, you can stay with a local family. Call the **Viet Hai Tourism Association** (☎ 031-888 836) for homestay information.

No roads lead to Viet Hai. If you're not up for following the treacherous trail from the national park headquarters, you can hire a boat at Cat Ba Town. It's an hour's ride from there to Viet Hai jetty, and another 45 minutes' walk through gentle terrain from there to the village. Food stalls and refreshment stands await your arrival.

🌀 HIEN HAO VILLAGE

On the coast road, about 20km northwest of Cat Ba Town, Hien Hao village offers another appealing rural alternative. It's a little hamlet of 400 souls surrounded by karst formations and rice paddies, and short hikes will get you into thick tropical forests or to scenic coastal overlooks. You can arrange an overnight stay with a local family, and use the town as a base for exploratory treks. For information contact the **Hien Hao Peoples Committee** (☎ 031-888 732).

🏠 SLEEP

🏠 CAT BA SUNRISE RESORT

☎ 031-887 360; Cat Co 3 Beach; r US$77-99, ste US$140-170
This four-star resort is tucked away on its own private beach, about 1km from Cat Ba Town. It has an attractive setting, with black cliffs rising behind it, a large pool and patio, a gym, a couple of restaurants and a bar on the beach. Guest rooms provide a taste of modern elegance.

🏠 HOLIDAY VIEW HOTEL

☎ 031-887 200; holidayviewhotel@vnn.vn; Đ 1-4, Cat Ba Town; d US$45-60
Away from the centre of Cat Ba Town, along the road that leads to the beaches, is this three-star high-rise hotel. Rooms are tidy, if minimalist, and services are a clear cut above the island's standards. The 12th-floor rooms with balconies offer spectacular views.

DRAGON TALES

'Halong' translates as 'descending dragons', which alludes to a Vietnamese legend that accounts for the unique topography of Halong Bay's coastline. According to this myth, the islands of the bay were formed by a family of great dragons that came down from the heavens, spitting up rock and gouging out valleys to ward off an invading navy. The dragons were apparently enamoured with the natural beauty of Halong Bay, and decided to stay rather than return to heaven.

TOURS OF PARADISE

An alarming number of tourist boats, many of them designed to resemble traditional Chinese junks, head out into Halong Bay every day, only to mysteriously disperse among the bay's secluded islands and coves. Clusters of boats tend to pull up together for the night, and it can be cheery to see their lights dance on the water and to hear voices echoing off the surrounding rock formations long after dark. Tours often include swimming, kayaking and short hikes. It's best to plan ahead, but if you haven't, it's easy to arrange a tour from Hanoi on just 24 hours notice.

Recommended tour operators:

Emeraude (Map pp68-9, E3; ☎ 04-934 0888; www.emeraude-cruises.com; Press Club, 59A Pho Ly Thai To, Hanoi; d per night US$310-330) The five-star Emeraude is a replica paddle steamer that exudes colonial luxury. The air-conditioned cabins are exquisitely designed with period furnishings; meals are of the highest standard; and a full range of services is available. You can order cocktails and have your feet massaged without ever leaving your deckchair, all while the graceful boat tools around the bay.

Handspan (Map pp42-3, F3; ☎ 04-926 0581, ext 101 or 102; www.handspan.com; 80 Pho Ma May, Hanoi; 1-night tours per person US$132-165) Vietnam's premier tour company offers a variety of alluring ways in which to enjoy Halong Bay. The boats are stylish and well maintained and the food and service are very good. Your fellow travellers probably won't be young backpackers. Handspan also offers a kayaking and camping trip that overnights on a private beach. These folks run a polished operation. The office is in the Tamarind Cafe, out the back. Check the website for details.

Open Tour Sinh Café (Map pp68-9, D3; ☎ 04-936 3577; www.sinhcafe.com.vn; 39 Hang Khay, Hanoi; 1-night tours per person from US$25) This outlet of Sinh Café, opposite Hoan Kiem Lake in the French Quarter, is staffed by friendly people who speak English and French. Most of the tours offered here are not as leisurely as those offered by Handspan, though some of the companies represented here do have three-star boats. The cheaper boats tend to attract a young and fun crowd.

Timing Your Trip

During winter Halong Bay can be enshrouded in fog and drizzle, and the water is cold and less enticing for swimming and kayaking. That's not to say the bay completely loses its appeal, however, as the topography takes on a beautiful and mysterious quality that, for some, is more alluring than in sunny weather. Just bear this in mind when making your plans. February and March are generally the gloomiest months.

HALONG BAY

🏠 PRINCES HOTEL

☎ 031-888 899; www.princeshotel
-catba.com; Cat Ba Town; r US$16-25

The best option in the centre of
Cat Ba Town is this modern hotel,
styled to look like a colonial palace.
It is half a block from the wharf. The
80 rooms are large and clean, and
the hotel has a restaurant, sauna
and billiards room, and a roof terrace where you can enjoy a drink.

🏠 TRA MY HOTEL

☎ 031-888 650; greenmangocatba@
yahoo.com; Đ 1-4, Cat Ba Town; r
US$16-20

This family-run hotel is representa-
tive of the majority of modern
hotels overlooking the port. It's a
little chintzy in terms of décor, but
rooms are clean and many have
balconies overlooking the bay. An
added bonus here, perhaps, are
the 'saucy' bathroom tiles. You'll
see what we mean.

EAT

🍴 GREEN MANGO

International $$

☎ 031-887 151; greenmangocatba@
yahoo.com; Đ 1-4, Cat Ba Town; ⏱ 6am-
midnight

Widely considered the best
all-around restaurant in Cat Ba
Town, Green Mango lures in many
a traveller with its frosty mugs
of cold beer. Western dishes are
prepared with contemporary flair

and quality ingredients, including
grass-fed beef and organic pro-
duce. The filet mignon is capably
handled, while the roast lamb
spring rolls are an intriguing East-
West hybrid.

🍴 HOANG Y

Seafood $

Đ 1-4, Cat Ba Town; ⏱ 5-10pm

Playing strictly to Cat Ba's
strengths, this waterfront kitchen
specialises in fresh seafood dishes,
which are served in heaping
helpings. It's a fun, no-frills sort of
place that generally draws a large,
friendly crowd. Shrimp or squid
grilled with garlic, steamed whole
fish with ginger sauce, and ice-
cold beers make for bright spirits.
The menu includes vegetarian
selections, too.

🍴 XUAN HONG

Seafood $$

☎ 031-888 485; Ben Beo Pier, Ben Beo;
⏱ 6-10pm

There are several floating restaurants just offshore that serve fresh
seafood. This place farms its own
fish, crabs, shrimps and other deli-
cacies, which you will see in the
cages just off the jetty. Place your
order and someone will come
out and pluck it from the cage. It
doesn't get any fresher. Ask your
hotel to arrange a boat taxi out to
the restaurant.

Fishing for crabs in the jade waters of the bay

 DRINK

FLIGHTLESS BIRD *Bar*

☎ 031-888 517; Đ 1-4, Cat Ba Town;
⏲ 6.30pm-late

An attractive little room, this Kiwi-owned bar has a sophisticated cocktail-lounge vibe to it. Mindful of its resort environs, however, its doors are generally flung wide open so patrons can watch the promenading tourists on hot nights. There are pool, darts, and smart tunes blasting from the stereo.

NOBLE HOUSE *Pub*

☎ 031-888 363; Đ 1-4, Cat Ba Town;
⏲ 8am-late

This pub's biggest attribute is its lively atmosphere, which generally spills out onto the pavement. If you're yearning for a game of darts or eight-ball, or hankering for basic Aussie pub grub, look no further.

HAIPHONG

Of Halong Bay's two embarkation points – Haiphong and Halong City – Haiphong is the one in which you'd least object to being marooned for a night. At its core is a surprisingly charming colonial port city, its wide avenues and French villas resembling a quieter version of Hanoi's French Quarter. Spreading out from the old centre,

Haiphong has grown into a modern industrial port. It's Vietnam's fourth-largest city.

Arriving from Hanoi, most tourists simply make their way to the hydrofoil pier and are done with Haiphong. If you're on a tight schedule, you'll want to do the same. If you have a day to spare, overnighting in Haiphong allows enough time to take in the city's sights. Hotels, services and sights are concentrated on Pho Dien Bien Phu. The ferry pier is just a few blocks north of here.

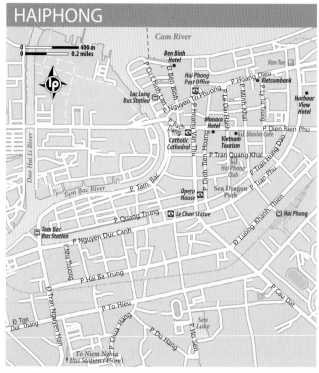

HAIPHONG

HAIPHONG IN WARTIME

In November 1946, as Vietnam's independence movement gained momentum, the French tossed a huge spark into the gasoline by bombarding the 'native quarters' of Haiphong. Hundreds of civilians – perhaps as many as 6000, according to some counts – were killed after a customs dispute incited a riot. Less than a decade later, the French withdrew from Indochina, with many boatloads of French troops departing from Haiphong Harbour.

During the American War, Haiphong was regularly bombed by US planes. In 1972, President Richard Nixon authorised the mining of the harbour. The war ended the following year and the mines were cleared out.

INFORMATION

You'll find internet cafés and ATMs on Pho Dien Bien Phu and elsewhere in the centre of town. **Vietcombank** (11 Pho Hoang Dieu) can change money. The lovely **Hai Phong Post Office** (3 Pho Nguyen Tri Phuong) is nearby. Tourist information is available at **Vietnam Tourism** (☎ 031-747 216; 55 Pho Dien Bien Phu; ◷ 8am-noon & 2-5pm), in the Thang Nam Hotel. Staff can arrange tours of Halong Bay and advise you on ways of getting back to Hanoi.

See www.haiphong.gov.vn for more information on Haiphong.

GETTING THERE & AROUND

The best way to get to Haiphong from Hanoi is by train – see p141 for details. Most of what you'd want to see in Haiphong is within a walkable area. You can catch *xe om* on most street corners. Tell drivers where you're headed, and negotiate the price before hopping on (a ride should cost from 10,000d to 20,000d). You can also hail a passing taxi, or call **Hai Phong Taxi** (☎ 031-841 999).

SEE

Historic architecture is Haiphong's appeal, so a leisurely walk around the old centre is the best way to appreciate the city. Follow Pho Dien Bien Phu west to Pho Hoang Van Thu, turn left, and then turn right onto Pho Quang Trung and you will see most of the city's highlights.

Hai Phong Post Office (3 Pho Nguyen Tri Phuong) was built in 1875. The **Catholic Cathedral** (cnr Pho Hoang Van Thu & Pho Tran Quang Khai) was built at the end of the 19th century and has been restored. The **Opera House** (Pho Quang Trung) has also been respectfully refurbished. If possible, enter for a look at its lavish interior. Pho Tran Hung Dao and its continuation, Pho Quang Trung, share a grassy median called **Sea Dragon Park**, which is pleasant for strolling. A **statue of Le Chan**, the military

HALONG BAY

A stroll around Haiphong will make you smile too

commander who oversaw the Trung Sisters' rebellion, is the focal point along this strip.

SLEEP

Tour groups from Europe and China often flood Haiphong's better hotels, so book ahead. In a pinch, tour agencies and hotels in Hanoi can very likely set you up in a decent, family-run minihotel.

BEN BINH HOTEL
☎ 031-842 260; fax 842 524; 6 Đ Ben Binh; d US$20-30
If you missed the hydrofoil to Cat Ba, Ben Binh awaits across the street from the pier. It's a huge old

hotel surrounded by lush gardens. Ask to look at a few rooms before checking in, as they're not all up to date.

HARBOUR VIEW HOTEL
☎ 031-827 827; www.harbourviewviet nam.com; 4 Pho Tran Phu; d US$80
Haiphong's best hotel, the Harbour View was designed to look like a colonial palace, and it follows through with stylish rooms. It also features a swimming pool, a gym and a spa.

MONACO HOTEL
☎ 031-746 468; monacohotel@vnn.vn; 103 Pho Dien Bien Phu; d US$25-50
The Monaco is a good choice, with smartly decorated rooms up from an impressive foyer. If you're exploring the town's architectural highlights, this hotel has a great central location.

EAT

Pho Tran Hung Dao, along Sea Dragon Park, is a great place to look for good local eateries, many of which set up tables out the front.

HAI PHONG CLUB
Vietnamese $$
☎ 031-822 603; 17 Pho Tran Quang Khai; ⊙ 8am-midnight
The décor is a little cheesy in this smart little supper club, but in a

good way. The food's not bad, but the place gets interesting after 9pm, when live musicians and cabaret singers perform.

⑪ MAXIM CAFE
Vietnamese $$

☎ 031-822 934; 51B Pho Dien Bien Phu;
🕐 8am-midnight

It's a good place to come for lunch or dinner, and even better for entertainment, which starts up after 8pm. Some nights it's classical music; others jazz or cabaret.

⑪ VAN TUE
Vietnamese seafood $

☎ 031-746 337; 1A Pho Hoang Dieu;
🕐 10am-11pm

This huge and modern banquet hall gets pretty festive at times, helped along by the Pilsner they brew here. The food, with a strong seafood bias, is good and gets better after a few rounds of those house suds. Head down to the basement or out to the garden for the best atmosphere.

Thanks to free enterprise, Hanoians have more income than ever before – new villas, restaurants and clubs are popping up all over town. With the added influx of tourist dollars, historic buildings are being restored, and aspects of culture once banned by the communists are permitted to flourish. It's an exciting time to visit.

Admiring the view over Bay Mau Lake, Lenin Park (p70)

ACCOMMODATION

Accommodation is easily arranged from home via the internet. Rates are commonly published in US dollars, and centrally located, family-run mini-hotels usually charge US$20 or less for a double room. Four- and five-star accommodation can climb to over US$100, but it's still much cheaper in Hanoi than in other, more developed countries. Service is generally quite good. Prices peak during the Christmas and Tet seasons. If you're heading out to Halong Bay, your best accommodation choices are aboard boats humble or grand, which can cost anywhere from US$25 to US$330 per night. Cat Ba and Haiphong have decent hotels, with rooms from US$20.

Even at the cheapest places in Hanoi, staff speak at least some English and/or French, and often wi-fi or internet terminals are available. In most hotels, laundry services, taxi bookings and water-puppet-show ticket purchases can be arranged through the front desk.

Before making a booking in Hanoi, figure out in which part of town you want to stay. Staying in the Old Quarter is the surest way to immerse yourself in the culture and life of a densely packed and bustling Asian city. Little effort is required to absorb the city, for the Old Quarter will simply absorb you. Step outside and you'll be pulled in the direction of good bars, street eats and twisting lanes. Budget-oriented, family-run minihotels are the mainstay in this part of town. They're usually nothing fancy, but the best ones have clean rooms, air-conditioning, internet access and helpful front desks. You'll find similar accommodation in the Nha Tho area, but the surrounding streets are not quite so intense or noisy as in the heart of the Old Quarter.

Need a place to stay? Find and book it at lonelyplanet .com. Around 40 properties are featured for Hanoi – each personally visited, thoroughly reviewed and happily recommended by a Lonely Planet author. From hostels to high-end hotels, we've hunted out the places that will bring you unique and special experiences. Read independent reviews by authors and other travel aficionados like you, and get practical information including amenities, maps and photos. Then reserve your room simply and securely via Haystack – our online booking service. It's all at www.lonelyplanet.com/accommodation.

If you require more peace and quiet, the large hotels of the French Quarter and West Lake may be your ticket. These parts of town host many five-star hotels that offer guests views of the city below. Converting villas into luxuriant B&Bs seems like a natural idea that hasn't yet caught on in Hanoi.

Around Halong Bay, landlubbers will find minihotels and snazzy resort digs on Cat Ba Island, with prices in the same range as in Hanoi. Haiphong is an attractive city that's somewhat lacking when it comes to distinctive accommodation, but decent places can be found around the centre of town.

When checking in, you will, typically, be asked to hand over your passport so that the hotel can register you at the local police station. Sometimes hotels will accept a photocopy, but more often than not they'll want to borrow your actual passport for an hour or so.

WEB RESOURCES
Useful websites:
Asia Hotels (www.asiahotels.com/hl/Hanoi-Vietnam.asp)
AsiaRooms.com (www.asiarooms.com/vietnam/hanoi-hotels.html)
Hotels in Vietnam (www.hotels-in-vietnam.com)

BEST OLD QUARTER DIGS
> Joy Hotel (www.hanoijoyhotel.com)
> Stars Hotel (email hoalinhhotel@hn
  .vnn.vn)
> Sunshine 1 Hotel (www.hanoisun
  shinehotel.com)
> Classic Street Hotel (email hohoa@hn
  .vnn.vn)
> Lucky Star Hotel (www.luckystarhotel
  .com)

BEST FOR OPULENCE
> Sofitel Metropole (www.sofitel-hanoi
  -vietnam.com)
> Hanoi Daewoo (www.hanoi-dae
  woohotel.com)
> Hilton Hanoi Opera (www.hanoi
  .hilton.com)
> Melia Hanoi (www.meliahanoi.com)
> Sheraton Hanoi (www.sheraton.com)

SNAPSHOTS

ARCHITECTURE

Despite the extraordinary pace of demolition and rebuilding, driven by Vietnam's rapidly growing economy, Hanoi remains a stunning city with a great variety of building types. The Chinese and the French have exerted their influence, as have local laws and functional requirements. The city's great hodgepodge of buildings is a delightful eyeful.

TUBE HOUSES

The traditional two-storey shop-houses of the Old Quarter are known as 'tube houses' due to their pencil-thin dimensions. They're long and narrow, owing to a long-expired law that determined property taxes according to the width of a building's façade. Many of these shop-houses measure a mere 3m wide, and some are as long as 50m. Typically they have open-face shopfronts and gently sloping gabled roofs layered with thick terracotta shingles. Courtyards and air wells make the back of the house and the upstairs rooms livable. Since the 1990s, many of the traditional tube houses have been replaced by modern, French-influenced shop-houses standing four or five storeys tall. These new houses are still limited to the original narrow lots, and often adhere to similar floor plans.

FRENCH-COLONIAL

Stately villas, Catholic churches and imposing government structures abound in the French Quarter and near Ba Dinh Sq. The villas typically exhibit adaptations to Hanoi's balmy climate, with balconies, wraparound porches and wide eaves to let in cool air while keeping out the rain and hot sun. Some colonial buildings incorporate imperial Asian features.

PAGODAS & TEMPLES

The Chinese influence is most visible in Hanoi's places of worship. Temples tend to comprise clusters of buildings around courtyards. Entry to these closed compounds is through a grand gate, and entry to the buildings often requires stepping over a raised threshold. Most notable are the swooping hip rafters and terracotta roof shingles.

BEST SPOTS TO ADMIRE HANOI ARCHITECTURE

> Cafe Pho Co's rooftop terrace (p53)
> KOTO's 'treetop terrace' (p92)
> ILU Lounge's window seat (p98)
> Club 51's extravagant interior (p74)
> Emperor's lush courtyard (p75)

BEST ARCHITECTURAL LANDMARKS

> 87 Ma May (p41; pictured above) – restored 19th-century tube house
> Hanoi Opera (p81) – French-colonial theatre
> History Museum (p67) – 'neo-Vietnamese' structure
> Ho Chi Minh Mausoleum (p84) – Soviet brutalism with traditional Vietnamese motifs
> Temple of Literature (p90) – ancient Chinese-influenced academic compound

DRINKING

Wherever in the world you go, you're bound to meet a few sozzled souls who enjoy a drink a little more than everybody else, and Hanoi is no exception. If Hanoi's boozeoisie is not world famous, it's because what they drink here is not suitable for export. But it's really about the context and the company, and within the friendly confines of Hanoi, the swill they're pouring is fine.

Bia hoi is the local draught brew. It's notable for its cheapness, and in some quarters the patrons will freely admit the beer is crap. Not all *bia hoi* joints serve a watery product, though, and some spots can provide you with exactly what you need on a hot day. The stuff nearly always benefits from the atmosphere, which usually involves a kerbside view of a chaotic street scene. No setting in Hanoi is so conducive to making friends with the locals as a good *bia hoi* joint.

Less appealing to foreigners is *ruou*, the local rice wine. Whether 'wine' is as accurate a translation as 'paint thinner' is a matter of debate. It's like moonshine sake, though it's not warmed. Vietnamese insist it enhances sexual potency, particularly when the liquor is infused with a dead cobra or an endangered species of some sort. Some very pleasant bottled *ruou*, lacking rare animals, are served at the Highway 4 bar (p51 and p75).

Table wine is produced in the wine-growing region of Dalat, but to most foreign palates these wines are considered inferior. Imports are becoming more widely available.

BEST BIA

> Lan Chin (p78)
> Bia Hoi 68 Hang Quat (p52)
> Quan Bia Minh (p54)
> Red Beer (p54)
> Legends Beer (p53)

BEST ADVICE FOR DRINKERS

> don't get drunk on *bia hoi*
> do order some Vietnamese peanuts – they make an excellent snack
> don't mix your *bia* and your *ruou*
> do say *'không cám ơn'* ('no thank you') if you're offered a mysterious drink in a clay jug with a wooden straw sticking out
> do order a bowl of *pho* (rice-noodle soup) if you have a hangover – it's the best treatment

Opposite Highway 4 (p51), a good spot to sample *ruou* **Above** What's your poison? *Ruou* on display in a city bar

FOOD

Vietnamese cuisine has earned a reputation for being satisfying, light, healthy and tasty. Most travellers are probably somewhat familiar with *pho bo* (beef noodle soup) and the variety of noodle and rice plates commonly available internationally. In Hanoi, you'll instantly realise that the good stuff you've had back home tastes even better here. You'll also discover many Hanoi specialities that rarely turn up on overseas menus.

The local cuisine is firmly rooted in its wonderful street stalls and one-dish mother-daughter eateries. Most of these joints are resolutely utilitarian in terms of atmosphere, but they are always the best places to get Hanoi favourites such as *bun cha* (rice vermicelli with barbecued pork and vegetables), *pho bo*, *banh cuon* (silky steamed rice crepes filled with minced pork, mushrooms and ground shrimp) and *banh ghoi* (patties filled with pork, glassy noodles, mushroom and seasonings). The Old Quarter swarms with street-food delights such as these.

More recent are the bounty of highly stylised cosmopolitan restaurants that conjure images of neocolonial luxury. Many an old French villa has been converted into a romantic restaurant. Some of these classy establishments serve up refined versions of the old street classics, while others draw upon a variety of international influences. The food is generally of a very high standard in these places, though it is sometimes overshadowed by the sumptuous atmosphere. The main drawback is that Vietnamese don't eat in these establishments. What's the point in coming to Hanoi just to hang out with other tourists?

The local dining scene is easy to grasp, even on a short visit. Food blogs are often the quickest inroad if you're doing a little pre-trip research. **Sticky Rice** (http://stickyrice.typepad.com) is probably the most informative, and has great links to other worthwhile sites. The online version of **Vietnam News** (http://vietnamnews.vnanet.vn) has regular restaurant reviews in English.

Ordering a meal in a restaurant is not complicated, because the more expensive restaurants have menus in English. Even some of the humbler places have English menus. In the one-dish restaurants, the name of the place (eg Pho Such-and-Such) often tells you what's available.

BEST LATE-NIGHT DINING
> Restaurant Bobby Chinn (p77)
> Chim Sao (p74)
> ILU Lounge (p98)
> La Salsa (p63)
> Tamarind Café (p52)

BEST HANOI DISHES
> *bun cha* – rice vermicelli with barbecued pork and vegetables
> *banh cuon* – silky steamed rice crepes filled with minced pork, mushrooms and ground shrimp
> *bo bay mon* – seven beef dishes
> *cha ca* – fish grilled with turmeric and dill, served with noodles and peanuts
> *nem ran* – spring rolls
> *pho bo* – beef noodle soup

Opposite Streetside dining beside Truc Bach Lake **Above** More little blue tables in the Old Quarter

KIDS

Hanoi offers many entertainments and activities that appeal to children, including daily water-puppet shows (see Thang Long Water Puppet Theatre, p55), and a Sunday morning circus performance that caters to kids (see Central Circus, p81). On sweltering days, take the young 'uns out to Ho Tay Water Park (p99), where they can splash in pools and on slides all day.

Your rambunctious little guys can shake off cabin fever by walking around Hoan Kiem Lake (p56), while Lenin Park (p70) offers more in terms of rides and activities. Paddleboats that look like geese will get the family out onto the water on Lenin Park's Bay Mau Lake. You'll find more goose-boats on Truc Bach Lake and West Lake. *Cyclos* (pedicabs or bicycle rickshaws) offer a fun way to get to any of these sites.

Children who travel frequently (and travel well) don't always need to be treated to kid-specific entertainments. Take them to museums such as the excellent Vietnam Museum of Ethnology (p86), where they can learn about Vietnam's unique ethnic cultures. A visit to the Ho Chi Minh Mausoleum (p84) is sure to spark stimulating conversations about Vietnam's history and the wars with the French and the Americans.

Anytime you need to sweeten the deal, Hanoi's ice creameries are there to help. Fanny (p62), Hanoi's best ice-cream shop, is a fun place where creative presentation of the desserts makes the eating all the more fun.

A boat tour of Halong Bay's hidden island grottoes and beaches (see the boxed text, p111) is a sure way to keep adventurous tykes happy. These excursions can include kayaking expeditions and time lazing away on sandy beaches.

BEST KID-FRIENDLY EATERIES
> Banh Cuon Gia Truyen (p48)
> Tamarind Café (p52)
> Fanny (p62)
> Quan An Ngon (p77)
> Cafe Smile (p92)

BEST SOUVENIRS FOR KIDS TO TAKE HOME
> wooden cricket instruments
> kid-sized conical hats
> exotic sweets
> evocative watercolour paintings (around US$2)
> wooden dolls

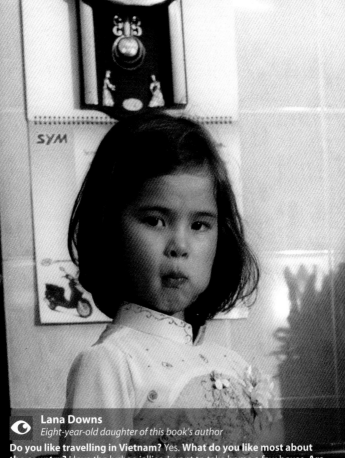

Lana Downs
Eight-year-old daughter of this book's author

Do you like travelling in Vietnam? Yes. **What do you like most about the country?** I love the lychee jellies. I want to take home a few boxes. **Are Vietnamese kids friendly?** Yes, and they're very curious. Some are learning English and want to ask me lots of questions.

MUSEUMS

It's museums galore in Hanoi, where many fascinating institutions detail the history, art and culture of the city and the nation. If you're in town for only a few days, you may have some difficult choices to make.

For anyone interested in Vietnam's lengthy struggle against the French and the Americans, Hanoi's museums offer a special bounty. Tops on the list are the Viet Nam Military History Museum (p85) and the Museum of the Vietnamese Revolution (p71). The Ho Chi Minh Museum (p84) and the Museum of Vietnamese Women (p71) also delve into the wars. All of these museums are government-owned and were originally intended to educate the Vietnamese people. The tone is generally nationalistic – you can easily imagine the voice of Hanoi Jane curating the exhibits – and in spots the captions could use more explanation for those foreigners who are less familiar with Vietnamese history. English-speaking guides can help you get the most out of a visit.

Less intense is the Vietnam Fine Arts Museum (p90), which exhibits art from ancient times on through the war years. The wartime art is strictly sympathetic with the northern cause, as you'd expect, but it's not pure propaganda (although propaganda art, which can be seen in shops that sell it, certainly has its aficionados). Some of the ancient treasures here are extraordinary, and they help fill some of the gaps left by the loss of so much traditional architecture and art during the endless wars.

Anthropology and ancient history are the primary thrusts of the History Museum (p67; pictured below), and ethnic cultures are celebrated at the excellent Vietnam Museum of Ethnology (p86).

MUSIC

Vietnamese pop music gets a bad rap in the Western world, probably because the Vietnamese language doesn't sound particularly lyrical to Western ears – and it can be hard to take when it's blasted through the heavy reverb so favoured by the Vietnamese. Local tastes are changing, though, as neocabaret vocalists give way to younger hip-hop-influenced singers and more serious and arty electronic artists.

Traditional Vietnamese folk music is far more soothing. It is generally performed acoustically in intimate environs, including some French Quarter restaurants and at the water-puppet shows. Standard instrumentation includes the *tam* lute (a wooden banjo with a snake-skin resonator) and the two-string *nhi* fiddle (which looks like a wooden spike jabbed into a wooden cup), along with a variety of percussion instruments. The unusual and melancholic *dan bau* (an electronic instrument much like a one-string steel guitar with a whammy bar) often features in solos. Music shops along Pho Hang Manh (Map pp42–3, D5) in the Old Quarter sell beautiful hand-carved folk instruments.

Some musical traditions were banned in 1954, at the end of colonial rule, but song forms such as *ca tru* are now being celebrated as part of the national heritage. *Ca tru* was traditionally sung by women in tea parlours patronised by the elite class, and its popularity peaked in the 15th century. Today it is sung in fairly formal salons (and at Ho Guom Audio – see p55). Most Hanoians will admit that *ca tru* can be a bit challenging, as it follows unusual rhythmic and tonal patterns. But it's very exotic, and the performances are a dramatic throwback to ancient Vietnam. *Ca hue* is another traditional style of music, originating in the city of Hué. It, too, can be a taste that only Vietnamese intellectuals take the trouble to acquire, and it's generally performed in intimate salons.

SHOPPING & MARKETS

Many visitors to Hanoi swarm the silk shops along the Old Quarter's Pho Hang Gai and Pho Hang Bong (Map pp42–3, D5). The silk produced in Vietnam is not considered the world's finest, but it's very inexpensive, and Vietnamese designers have a fun and flowery sensibility that appeals to foreigners. Some of the city's best boutiques are to be found along Pho Nha Tho (Map p57, B3) and Nha Chung (Map p57, B4), just west of Hoan Kiem Lake. Women will find original designer clothing, handbags, jewellery and other fashion accessories along these corridors.

Hanoi is also a great city in which to purchase art and decorative crafts for your home. The city's burgeoning gallery scene is not strictly geared towards serious collectors; the greater appeal is for those with a casual appreciation for art. Hanoi has a wealth of highly trained and talented painters whose work sells relatively cheaply. See pp12–13 for information about galleries.

Ethnic crafts are also worth seeking out – the intricately woven textiles of the Black Thai, Pathen and H'mong are often beautiful enough to frame or hang as tapestries. Also look for H'mong batik patterns. Many of these tribes are also known for their basketry and pottery.

Hanoi's public markets are always worth touring, although the goods sold here address the everyday needs of less-affluent locals rather than tourists. These markets are often great for sampling tropical fruits and picking up inexpensive knock-offs from China. Dong Xuan Market (p41) also has a squadron of tailors who can mark up and cut a suit in a day or two.

BEST FASHION SHOPS
> Song (p61)
> Ipa-Nima (p59)
> Kenly Silk (p47)
> Cocoon (p58)
> L'Image (p59)

BEST NON-SOUVENIR SOUVENIRS
> ethnic tapestries, suitable for hanging
> paintings
> silk *ao dai* (Vietnamese national dress)
> musical instruments
> propaganda posters

>BACKGROUND

Paying respects at the Ambassadors' Pagoda (p67)

BACKGROUND

HISTORY

The site where Hanoi stands has been inhabited since the Neolithic period. The city's illustrious history has had its spurts and lulls, beginning with a successful revolt against the Chinese in the 6th century AD, when King Ly Bi established the capital at a site near West Lake. Ly Bi then ordered the building of Tran Quoc Pagoda (p96), which still exists, although with rebuilt structures. The capital was soon moved out to Co Loa, northeast of the pagoda, and the Chinese reasserted control after a few decades.

In 1010 Emperor Ly Thai To established a walled citadel in present-day Hanoi. Sixty years later, Emperor Ly Thanh Tong founded the Temple of Literature (p90), which became the country's first university. For centuries, future mandarins received their doctorates here.

Beyond the citadel walls and beside the Red River, a commercial district took shape in what is now the Old Quarter. This area first formed as a marketplace, with vendors and craftspeople from surrounding villages pulling up their carts and setting up stalls here. By the 13th century, the Quarter had become a permanent settlement that was home to 36 guilds, each claiming (and naming – see the boxed text, p45) their own streets. The neighbourhood is still commonly known as 'the 36 streets', although its streets actually number over 50.

Europeans made sporadic contact for centuries, until Franciscan and Jesuit missionaries arrived in the 16th century. An English attempt to establish trade links was foiled in 1613, when an agent of the East India Company was murdered in Hanoi.

In 1802 Emperor Gia Long, founder of the Nguyen dynasty, decided to rule from Hué, thus relegating Hanoi to the status of a regional capital. It would remain as such for 100 years.

OPIUM IN INDOCHINA

Indochina was not a profitable colony for the French until Paul Doumer became governor general in 1897. Part of Doumer's success came from the opium trade, which he introduced to the colony. Opium was not widely used by the Vietnamese people until Doumer opened a refinery and sanctioned the distribution throughout the country. The sale of opium, which quickly grew in popularity, eventually covered one-third of the cost of administrating the colony.

In the early 19th century, the Nguyen emperors attempted to expel French missionaries, and the murder of several Catholic clergymen provoked military action from France. The French attacked Danang in 1858, and they took Saigon (now known as Ho Chi Minh City) the following year. In 1862 Emperor Tu Duc relinquished control of Cochinchina (in the Mekong Delta), which the French claimed as a colony five years later. In 1872, in an unauthorised act, merchant Jean Dupuis seized the Hanoi citadel. Captain Francis Garnier took over from there, capturing the entire city before being killed by an insurgent group called the Black Flags. It took 10 years for the French to establish firm control over Hanoi, which became the capital of French Indochina in 1902.

Insurgencies continued to badger the French, and Hanoi's Maison Centrale (Hoa Lo Prison; p67) was built in part to incarcerate Vietnamese dissidents. By the 1930s Maison Centrale was filled to five times its designed capacity. The guillotine saw frequent use. In 1925 Ho Chi Minh founded the Revolutionary Youth League, which quickly evolved into the Vietnamese Communist Party.

During WWII the Vichy government accepted Japanese troops in Vietnam. The Viet Minh, formed by Ho in 1941, received arms and funding from the US Office of Strategic Services (OSS) and resisted Japanese occupation for the duration of the war.

By early 1945, as Japanese defeat became imminent, the Viet Minh gained control over much of northern Vietnam. On 2 September Ho declared Vietnamese independence at a large rally on Ba Dinh Sq.

The French attempt to re-establish their colony, and the eight-year Franco–Viet Minh War, resulted in the Geneva Accords of 1954, which split Vietnam into a pro-Western South and a communist North. Hanoi was established as the capital of North Vietnam.

The Hanoi government quickly instituted land reform, and executed or imprisoned thousands of citizens during its first few years in power. It also began, in 1959, its campaign to liberate the South, which set in motion events leading to the armed struggle with the US. During the American War Hanoi was regularly bombed by American jets. In the late 1960s and early 1970s Hoan Kiem Lake was ringed by concrete bomb shelters.

After the war ended, the Hanoi government forcibly reunified Vietnam, but the country was beset by economic collapse and famine. During the time of subsidy (1975–86), the citizens of Hanoi were allotted small rations of rice and vegetables. Inflation rendered the dong virtually

AKA HANOI

Hanoi has gone by many names through its long history. The Chinese called it Tong Binh after making it the capital of Annam in AD 679. The name later changed to Dai La, and after 1010 Emperor Ly Thai To renamed it Thang Long (City of the Soaring Dragon). The city was later renamed Dong Kinh (Eastern Capital) – the Europeans morphed this into Tonkin, and applied the name to all of northern Vietnam. The city was named Hanoi (City in the River Bend) by Emperor Tu Duc in 1831.

worthless. In 1986, following the lead of the USSR's *perestroika,* Hanoi initiated economic reforms known as Doi Moi. The government opened the economy, permitting free enterprise and foreign investment. Since the mid-1990s the economy has been growing steadily, bringing about rapid social change to Hanoi (made visible by the city's evolving skyline). For more details, see Economy, below.

ECONOMY

Vietnam's economy has grown spectacularly over the past decade, as the country has shifted its emphasis from agriculture to manufacturing. Key to this shift has been the policy of Doi Moi (meaning 'renovation'), through which the communist government relinquished its iron grip on the economy. This allowed a free-enterprise, market-driven economy to flourish. By and large, the Vietnamese people – well educated and entrepreneurial in spirit – have demonstrated ready adaptability to these changes. Vietnam's GDP has increased steadily since 1995, generally at a rate of over 7% per year.

This recent growth comes despite Vietnam's standing start when Doi Moi was instituted in 1986. At the time, Vietnam was among the poorest countries in Asia, with very little capital with which to spur its own growth. Soviet aid dried up shortly thereafter. In 1994 renewed diplomatic relations with the US helped initiate foreign investment and trade.

While Ho Chi Minh City is typically touted as being quicker on the draw, Hanoi has been no slouch. The city's GDP has grown at an average of 11% since 2002. Foreign investment has spurred new industries in high-end products, and international companies have been attracted by Vietnam's well-educated and relatively cheap labour force. Canon has built its largest laser-printer factory near Hanoi, and tech companies such as Intel have established plants. Vietnam's acceptance into the World

DOI MOI

Vietnam's economic reform, Doi Moi, was introduced in 1986 and was inspired in part by Mikhail Gorbachev's *perestroika*, but with a key difference. While the USSR's political reform (*glasnost*) accompanied the economic reform, in Vietnam the changes are purely economic. Vietnam is still ruled by one party, and political dissent is forbidden.

Trade Organization in 2006 is likely to encourage more foreign investment. At the same time, Vietnam's new wealthy class has proved adept at playing the stock market, so many Hanoians are reinvesting their fortunes in the country's growth. And in return, as the stock market soars, they're being amply rewarded.

One can see evidence of Hanoi's new-found prosperity all over town, as new restaurants and nightclubs catering to the local middle class open every week. Bicycles were supplanted years ago by faster, more expensive motorbikes, and imported cars – status symbols that are clearly impractical in Hanoi – are turning up in greater numbers. Those 'KCBT' signs spray-painted on buildings all over town are phone numbers of demolition crews, who are obviously getting a lot of work as the newly wealthy tear down their humble old tube houses (see p122) and replace them with five-storey villas.

However, Vietnam remains quite poor, and a widening income gap is creating new problems. More than one-fifth of the nation's population still lives below the poverty line. New jobs and higher incomes are concentrated in the cities, so, in recent years, Hanoi has seen a huge influx of poor people from nearby villages. Crime, while not a huge problem, is on the rise, as are prostitution and drug use.

Ever since Vietnam opened its doors to the outside world in the late 1980s, tourism has been a constantly growing sector of the economy. Despite the country's dramatic and rapid changes, some semblance of tradition is maintained in central Hanoi for the sake of tourists, many of whom come to see the charmed colonial capital. With tourism being so important, Hanoi does an impressive balancing act of moving forward while preserving much of its 19th-century elegance.

RELIGION

In Vietnam, Mahayana Buddhism, Confucianism and Taoism fused over the centuries to create a complex belief system sometimes referred to as the Tam Giao (Triple Religion). The majority of the population has a fairly relaxed familiarity with Buddhist doctrines, but if asked about religion, most Hanoians would probably say they are Buddhist. People often invite monks to participate in funerals, and pagodas are generally regarded as venerable places. When it comes to family or civic duties, Vietnamese are likely to follow the moral and social code of Confucianism. Many turn to Taoist concepts to understand the nature of the cosmos.

Religion is omnipresent, with temples turning up on nearly every block, and small shrines to ancestors appearing in shops and homes all over the city. Many Hanoians observe rites and traditions for good luck and out of respect for their ancestors.

Vietnam's constitution proclaims religious freedom, and yet religious practice was suppressed by the communists from the 1950s until 1989, when the government decided to relax its stance. Still, you aren't likely to see monks in great numbers walking the streets in Hanoi, and even many temples and pagodas are surprisingly monk-free.

Christianity was introduced to Vietnam in the 16th century, and took root over the ensuing centuries. In Asia, only the Philippines has more Christians. As a European import, Christianity was viewed with suspicion by the communists, and many Catholics migrated south after 1954, leaving the country altogether after 1975. However, nearly 10% of the population of Vietnam is Catholic, and Hanoi's landmark cathedrals have been slowly coming back to life over the past two decades.

ARTS

PAINTING

Painting on frame-mounted silk dates from the 13th century and was for a long time the preserve of scholar-calligraphers, who painted grand natural scenes. At the Ecole des Beaux-Arts d'Indochine, opened in Hanoi in 1925, local artists adopted expressive, European-influenced styles. Cross-cultural fusions resulted in impressionistic watercolours applied on silk canvases, as well as lacquer paintings of an artistic, rather than decorative, nature.

For many decades, art in Hanoi was restricted to political themes. Notable students of the Ecole des Beaux-Arts switched thematic emphasis from placid scenes of girls in *ao dai* (Vietnamese national dress) to nationalistic scenes of soldiers and patriots contributing to the independence movement and to the reunification effort.

DUONG THU HUONG

Among Hanoi's leading literary figures is Duong Thu Huong, a former member of the Communist Party who was declared a dissident after publishing several ground-breaking novels in the late 1980s and early '90s. Her novels frequently include characters who reflect the hypocrisy and selfishness of Communist Party members. Her *Paradise of the Blind* (1988) was the first novel from Vietnam to be published in the USA. *Beyond Illusions* (1987) and *Novel Without a Name* (1991) have also been translated into English and are widely available outside Vietnam. In 1991 Duong was imprisoned for seven months, and her novels are no longer available in her home country.

The economic reform of the last two decades has opened the floodgates to a swarm of well-trained artists now free to paint commercially oriented works. The relaxed environment has also made it possible for serious artists to explore personal and social themes. For a heads-up on Hanoi's gallery scene, see p12.

LITERATURE

Draconian censorship arrested the literature of Hanoi for much of the 20th century. Socialist realism, sanctioned by the government, limited writers to a select few subjects and a nationalistic point of view. In the mid-1980s Doi Moi (see p136) ushered in a new era. Local writers such as Nguyen Huy Thiep and Duong Thu Huong (see the boxed text, above) quickly set about publishing honest works that often cast a critical light on contemporary society and politics. The reform has its obvious limitations, however, as books are still frequently banned, and some of the country's leading literary figures have been silenced. More-recent works have pressed less directly against the Communist Party and are more open to interpretation.

THEATRE & PUPPETRY

Vietnamese theatre fuses music, singing, recitation, dance and mime. Classical Vietnamese theatre is strongly influenced by Chinese opera. Traditional forms such as *hat tuong* are fading, but modern folk opera has retained some of its popularity by introducing electronic instruments and contemporary themes.

Far more popular with tourists, however, are the water puppets, which have come back from the brink of extinction. Water puppetry began in

CINEMATIC HOMEWORK

Prior to your trip, pop the following flicks into your DVD player. Not all take place in Hanoi, but all make for excellent pre-trip watching.

The Quiet American (2002) A faithful adaptation of Graham Greene's excellent novel, set in 1950s Saigon, which more closely resembles postcolonial Hanoi.

Indochine (1993) Visually stunning French flick, a beauty contest between Catherine Deneuve and Halong Bay.

The Lover (1992) Interesting not just for the soft-porn scenes. Inverts the typical colonial dynamic in depicting a poor French girl's relationship with a wealthy Chinese man in the Mekong Delta.

At the Height of Summer (2000) Set in a peaceful Hanoi home, in which trouble brews beneath the surface.

Apocalypse Now (1979) Francis Ford Coppola's overproduced war extravaganza approximates the overblown indulgence of the war itself.

the Red River Delta in the 12th century. The art form was nearly dead in the early 1980s, when a government-sponsored movement restored it as part of the national heritage. As with the theatre, music and mythology are an integral part of water-puppet performances.

CINEMA

In 2002 the Ministry of Culture permitted private studios to form in Vietnam, and films that appeal to today's audiences are showing some promise. The biggest sensation thus far has been *Bar Girls* (2003), set in Ho Chi Minh City. Internationally, Vietnamese cinema has yet to make much of a splash, although Paris-based film-maker Tran Anh Hung enjoyed great art-house success in the 1990s. Tran's *À la verticale de l'été* (At the Height of Summer; 2000), set just a few years ago in Hanoi, portrays a much quieter and slower-paced city than you'll experience today.

DIRECTORY
TRANSPORT
ARRIVAL & DEPARTURE
AIR

All international flights arrive at **Noi Bai International Airport** (☎ 886 6527), some 35km north of the city. Direct flights from the west are nonexistent, and often you'll be transferring from your host airline to a Vietnam Airlines aircraft somewhere else in Asia, such as Hong Kong, Taipei or Bangkok.

Noi Bai is not a large or busy airport, and getting out of it is generally hassle-free. The airport currency-exchange bureau offers a fair exchange rate, and the taxi rank is just outside the terminal. The only sensible way from the airport to central Hanoi is by taxi, but before letting a cabbie take your luggage, make sure they charge a fixed rate of 150,000d, including the bridge toll. The ride takes 45 to 60 minutes.

TRAIN

In all likelihood, you'll only be taking the train if you're headed to Halong Bay and abhor the thought of taking a tour. Two trains depart daily from **Hanoi train station** (Map p89, D3; ☎ 942 2770, 942 3949; www.vr.com.vn; 120 Đ Le Duan), bound for Haiphong, at 6am and 3pm. The cost is around 17,000d one way and it takes about 2½ hours. In Haiphong the station is on Đ Luong Khanh Thien, a few blocks southeast of the ferry pier. See the Halong Bay chapter (p101) to plan the rest of your trip.

VISA

Tourist visas are required for all foreign visitors to Vietnam, and must be arranged through a Vietnamese consulate. Ideally, you should arrange your visa as soon as you've finalised your itinerary, but in reality the processing of your visa should take only a few days, at the most.

CLIMATE CHANGE & TRAVEL

Travel – especially air travel – is a significant contributor to global climate change. At Lonely Planet, we believe that all who travel have a responsibility to limit their personal impact. As a result, we have teamed with Rough Guides and other concerned industry partners to support Climate Care, which allows people to offset the greenhouse gases they are responsible for with contributions to energy-saving projects and other climate-friendly initiatives in the developing world. Lonely Planet offsets all staff and author travel.

For more information, turn to the responsible travel pages on www.lonelyplanet.com. For details on offsetting your carbon emissions and a carbon calculator, go to www.climatecare.org.

DEPARTURE TAX

A departure tax of US$14 is charged to all travellers leaving Noi Bai airport. Sometimes this tax is included in the price of your airline ticket – if not, pay the fee at the departure-fees desk before checking in.

GETTING AROUND

Most sites that are of interest to a traveller are concentrated in or near the Hoan Kiem District, which includes the Nha Tho area, the Old Quarter and the French Quarter. It's easy to walk around this district. More-outlying landmarks, such as the Ho Chi Minh Mausoleum, West Lake and the Temple of Literature, are all within a few blocks of this central district. To get from point A to point B quickly, you can always hail a taxi, *xe om* (pronounced say-*ome*; motorbike taxi) or *cyclo* (pedicab or bicycle rickshaw).

TAXI

Taxis are a common sight in Hoan Kiem District, especially around the lake. Some cabbies avoid the Old Quarter during peak commute times, and you may want to avoid taxis for the same reason. They don't move through traffic as easily as do the far more agile motorbikes. That said, taxis are very reasonably priced, and often make sense for parties of two or more. Fares within Hoan Kiem District go

Transport Times

	Old Quarter	Hoan Kiem Lake	French Quarter
Old Quarter	n/a	walk 5min; cyclo 3min; taxi/*xe om* 2min	walk 10min; cyclo 7min; taxi/*xe om* 5min
Hoan Kiem Lake	walk 5min; cyclo 3min; taxi/*xe om* 2min	n/a	walk 5min; cyclo 3min; taxi/*xe om* 2min
French Quarter	walk 10min; cyclo 7min; taxi/*xe om* 5min	walk 5min; cyclo 3min; taxi/*xe om* 2min	n/a
Ba Dinh	walk 20min; cyclo 15min; taxi/*xe om* 8min	walk 20min; cyclo 15min; taxi/*xe om* 8min	walk 20min; cyclo 15min; taxi/*xe om* 8min
Dong Da	walk 30min; cyclo 20min; taxi/*xe om* 12min	walk 15min; cyclo 10min; taxi/*xe om* 8min	walk 15min; cyclo 10min; taxi/*xe om* 8min
West Lake	walk 10min; cyclo 8min; taxi/*xe om* 5min	walk 25min; cyclo 17min; taxi/*xe om* 13min	walk 30min; cyclo 20min; taxi/*xe om* 15min

from 20,000d to 60,000d. Hotels and restaurants can call a taxi for you.

Recommended companies:
City Taxi (☎ 822 2222)
Noi Bai Taxi (☎ 886 5615, 927 2013)
Red Taxi (☎ 856 8686)

XE OM

'Xe' is short for *xe moto* (motorbike), and *'om'* means hold on for dear life. If you're travelling solo, these motorbike taxis are easily your best option. You'll quickly observe that most people get around town on motorbikes, and, considering the city's intensifying traffic, these slender vehicles make the most sense of all the available transport options. (Imagine the gridlock if every motorbike was to be replaced by a Ford Ranger.)

There are guys on nearly every corner willing to take you a few blocks or clear across the city for 10,000d to 20,000d. Most are completely trustworthy – but once you find a driver you can trust, stick with him.

Almost all *xe om* drivers are independent. Companies have begun to form that may one day take over the business, but at this point it's most convenient just to stroll down to the nearest corner and hire whoever is stationed there. Usually you'll have your choice of three or four aces, and at least one of them will strike you as likable and reasonable.

Ba Dinh	Dong Da	West Lake
walk 20min; cyclo 15min; taxi/*xe om* 8min	walk 30min; cyclo 20min; taxi/*xe om* 12min	walk 10min; cyclo 8min; taxi/*xe om* 5min
walk 20min; cyclo 15min; taxi/*xe om* 8min	walk 20min; cyclo 15min; taxi/*xe om* 8min	walk 25min; cyclo 17min; taxi/*xe om* 13min
walk 20min; cyclo 15min; taxi/*xe om* 8min	walk 20min; cyclo 15min; taxi/*xe om* 8min	walk 30min; cyclo 20min; taxi/*xe om* 15min
n/a	walk 10min; cyclo 7min; taxi/*xe om* 4min	walk 20min; cyclo 15min; taxi/*xe om* 10min
walk 10min; cyclo 7min; taxi/*xe om* 4min	n/a	walk 35min; cyclo 25min; taxi/*xe om* 20min
walk 20min; cyclo 15min; taxi/*xe om* 10min	walk 35min; cyclo 25min; taxi/*xe om* 20min	n/a

NEGOTIATING XE OM FARES

Most *xe om* (motorbike taxi) drivers speak enough English to settle on a price, often omitting the 'thousand' part. So '10' means '10,000d'. Some will ask for 50,000d, which is just their way of seeing how gullible you are.

Negotiating in dong rather than dollars is definitely the way to go, better yet in Vietnamese. A reliable approach is to start by offering 10 (or *muoi* – pronounced *muy*-ee), which will generally get you a nod of agreement. If you're going across two or three districts, the price will go up. *Moui-nam* (some Hanoians say this as *muoi-lam*) is 15; *hai-muoi* is 20.

Sometimes, after dropping you off, your driver will offer to wait and take you back to your hotel or on to your next destination. You can also negotiate a price for hiring the *xe om* and driver for a few hours, with several stops thrown in. It's like having a two-wheeled chauffeur. It helps to know some Vietnamese if you're negotiating a complicated deal.

CYCLO

Sadly, the *cyclo* (pedicab or bicycle rickshaw) has fallen from favour with Hanoians, and it is now a quaint throwback used mainly by tourists. *Cyclos* lurch through traffic at a leisurely pace, and if you're not averse to making yourself conspicuous, the ride can be quite pleasurable. You'll find them throughout the Old Quarter and around Hoan Kiem Lake. Usually a few cluster around French Quarter hotels and major tourist sites. You can negotiate set fares much as you would for a *xe om* (see the boxed text, above). Hiring a driver for an hour will allow enough time to tour the Old Quarter and loop around Hoan Kiem Lake. Fares are about 30,000d to 40,000d per hour, more if two are sharing the *cyclo*. Staff at your hotel may be able to help negotiate a fair price for you.

PRACTICALITIES
BUSINESS HOURS

Most shops operate from 8am to 6pm (give or take), seven days a week. Some shut down for an hour or two during the middle of the day, but this practice is becoming passé. Government-operated museums and tourist sights tend to take the day off on Monday. The rest of the week they open from 8am to 4pm or 5pm, with a long midday siesta (usually 11.30am to 1.30pm or 2pm). Many restaurants serve three meals a day, from 6am or 7am to 9pm or 10pm. Some *bun cha* (rice vermicelli with barbecued pork and vegetables) vendors specialise in lunch, while some posh French Quarter establishments open only for lunch and dinner. A few *pho* (rice-noodle soup) joints close down by 10.30am or 11am.

ELECTRICITY

Electrical voltage is 220V. This means quick recharge times for laptops and MP3 players, but if your appliances were built for 110V, it's wise to make sure they have built-in power adaptors and surge protection before you plug in. Most sockets in Hanoi accommodate two-pinned plugs with round prongs, but many will also fit US-style flat-prong plugs.

EMERGENCIES

Hanoi is reasonably safe as far as big cities go, although drug use and youth violence are on the rise. Guns are virtually nonexistent – believe it or not, swords are the weapon of choice. Riding a *xe om* can make you vulnerable to having loosely held bags snatched, but the occurrence of such thefts is not high. Police officers in avocado-green uniforms can be found all over the place. If you need to call the police, dial ☎ 113, and for an ambulance call ☎ 115.

The following clinics provide medical and dental care on a par with Western clinics. They can arrange to transfer you to another country, if need be.

Family Medical Practice Hanoi (☎ 843 0748; Van Phuc Compound, 298 Pho Kim Ma, Ba Dinh District; ☾ 24hr for emergencies)

International SOS (Map pp68–9, C3; ☎ 934 0666; www.internationalsos.com; Central Bldg, 31 Pho Hai Ba Trung, Hoan Kiem District; ☾ 24hr)

HOLIDAYS

New Year's Day 1 January
Anniversary of the Founding of the Vietnamese Communist Party 3 February
Liberation Day 30 April
International Workers' Day 1 May
Ho Chi Minh's Birthday 19 May

BIRD FLU

Vietnam is one of 12 countries worldwide in which humans have contracted the H5N1 subtype of avian influenza. So far the disease has affected only rural parts of the country. Nearly 100 cases were reported between 2003 and 2005, after which the disease dropped off significantly. A new outbreak was reported in early 2007. Travellers to Hanoi are not at the highest risk unless they visit farms outside the city (not a recommended activity). As a general precaution, make sure all meat and eggs from poultry are well cooked before you eat. Before your trip it is wise to check online health advisories:

Australia (www.dfat.gov.au/travel)
Canada (www.travelhealth.gc.ca)
New Zealand (www.mfat.govt.nz/travel)
UK (www.doh.gov.uk/traveladvice)
US (www.cdc.gov/travel)

Buddha's Birthday Eighth day of the fourth moon (usually June)
National Day 2 September
Christmas Day 25 December

INTERNET

Internet cafés are all over Hanoi, and many hotels offer wi-fi access or terminals off the lobby. As part of your pre-trip planning, you may want to check out these useful and interesting sites:

AsiaRooms.com (www.asiarooms.com)
New Hanoian (www.newhanoian.com)
Noodle Pie (www.noodlepie.com)
Sticky Rice (http://stickyrice.typepad.com)
Things Asian (www.thingsasian.com)
Viet World Kitchen (http://vietworldkitchen .com)
Vietnam Investment Review (www.vir.com .vn/Client/TimeOut/default.asp)
Vietnam News (http://vietnamnews.vnanet.vn)

LANGUAGE
BASICS

Hello.	*Xin chào.*
Goodbye.	*Tạm biệt.*
How are you?	*Có khỏe không?*
Fine, thank you.	*Khỏe, cám ơn.*
Excuse me.	*Xin lỗi.*
Yes.	*Vâng.*
No.	*Không.*
Please.	*Làm ơn.*
Thank you (very much).	*Cảm ơn (rất nhiều).*
You're welcome.	*Không có chi.*
Do you speak English?	*Bạn có nói được tiếng Anh không?*
I don't understand.	*Tôi không hiểu.*

EATING & DRINKING

That was delicious!	*Ngon tuyệt!*
I'm a vegetarian.	*Tôi là người ăn chay.*
Please bring the bill.	*Xin mang hóa đơn.*

SHOPPING

How much is this?	*Bao nhiêu vậy?*
That's too expensive.	*Cái đó quá đắt.*

EMERGENCIES

I'm sick.	*Tôi bị đau.*
Help!	*Cứu tôi!*
Call the police!	*Làm ơn gọi công an!*
Call an ambulance!	*Làm ơn gọi xe cứu thương!*

DAYS & NUMBERS

today	*tối nay*
tomorrow	*ngày mai*
yesterday	*hôm qua*

1	*một*
2	*hai*
3	*ba*
4	*bốn*
5	*năm*
6	*sáu*
7	*bảy*
8	*tám*
9	*chín*
10	*mười*
11	*mười một*
19	*mười chín*

20	*hai mươi*
21	*hai mươi mốt*
22	*hai mươi hai*
30	*ba mươi*
90	*chín mươi*
100	*một trăm*
200	*hai trăm*
1000	*một nghìn*

MONEY

CURRENCY

The currency of Vietnam is the dong, with the smallest banknote being the virtually worthless 200d note. ATMs typically dispense 100,000d notes, which sometimes makes it impossible to make change for small businesses and food stalls, so take every opportunity to accumulate 1000d, 2000d and 5000d notes and coins and distribute them wisely. The largest notes, 50,000d and 100,000d (worth about US$3 and US$6, respectively), will be accepted grudgingly in high-end boutique shops, restaurants and hotels (most of which accept credit cards anyway).

Many businesses will accept US dollars, and some seem to prefer them. Where prices are offered in both dong and dollars, the conversion generally works against the traveller with dollars, though not always significantly.

You'll find ATMs with international links around Hoan Kiem Lake and the French Quarter. The currency-exchange counter at the airport offers fair exchange rates.

COSTS

In most cities, the sky's the limit when it comes to spending, but in Hanoi you can pull out all the stops for around US$200 a day (including accommodation). In truth, though, it isn't necessary to spend as much as that – many of

A LOT OF DONG

In Hanoi you'll have to get used to carrying around large wads of paper money. Break a 100,000d note, equivalent to about US$6, and you're likely to receive a hefty roll of tattered 2000d and 5000d notes in change.

There's a long story behind this. To keep it short: the French colonial currency, the piastre, was replaced in 1954 by the dong, which then followed different courses in the North and the South. In 1977 all currency in Vietnam was replaced by a new reunification dong. Thereafter, inflation rapidly eroded the dong's value. In a 1985 currency reissue, old dong were swapped at an exchange of 10:1 in favour of a new dong, but another round of hyperinflation deflated the new currency yet again. The standard ATM withdrawal today is one million dong, so you can safely assume that any Westerner you meet in Hanoi is a millionaire, with the cash to prove it.

the city's best eating and entertainment options are practically free. The only major variable is shopping, in which case the sky really is the limit.

NEWSPAPERS & MAGAZINES

The bookshops on Pho Trang Tien (Map pp68–9, D3) in the French Quarter often have English-language periodicals such as the *Vietnam Investment Review,* which includes the highly readable *Timeout* supplement with cultural articles and listings for Hanoi and Ho Chi Minh City. Nearly as good is the *Guide,* a supplement included within the *Vietnam Economic Times. Viet Nam News* is a reliable English-language daily with in-depth restaurant reviews. You can often borrow copies of these and other rags in expatriate cafés and bars, to peruse over a drink.

PHOTOGRAPHY & VIDEO

Kodak and Fuji processing centres proliferate around the Hoan Kiem District, especially along Pho Hang Khay and Pho Ba Trieu (Map pp68–9, D3), south of the lake. Rates are about 1500d per print and the quality is equivalent to what you'd receive in a commercial shop anywhere. You can also buy film in these shops. Batteries and memory cards are widely available wherever you

see window displays of digital cameras and camcorders. If you're still shooting film, **Nguyen Long** (Map pp68-9, C3; ☎ 826 6433; 17A Pho Ba Trieu) does processing and prints at a reasonable price and also provides a range of digital services.

TELEPHONE

Vietnam's cellular network uses GSM 900/1800. If you are from North America your mobile phone (cellphone) will not work in Vietnam. If you're coming from Australia, Europe or most of Asia and have a global-roaming device you can use your mobile in Hanoi. However, local calls with your mobile will be absurdly expensive unless you purchase a SIM card with a local Hanoi number. Look for these cards at shops that sell mobile phones. Such shops are everywhere.

If you do not have a mobile you can make international calls at the **main post office** (Buu Dien Ha Noi; Map pp68-9, D2; ☎ 825 4403; Pho Dinh Tien Hoang, French Quarter). It's easy to find, in the huge, highly visible building overlooking Hoan Kiem Lake.

COUNTRY, CITY & REGIONAL CODES

Throughout this guide, area codes have been included only for telephone numbers outside Hanoi.

Cat Ba Island	☎ 031
Haiphong	☎ 031

Halong Bay	☎ 033
Hanoi	☎ 04
Vietnam	☎ 84

USEFUL PHONE NUMBERS

| International direct dial code | ☎ 00 |
| Local directory inquiries | ☎ 1080 |

TIPPING

Tipping is not commonly expected. In some instances it's frowned upon by locals who do not want tipping to become compulsory, the way it has in other cultures. Some French Quarter restaurants have adopted the custom of *'service compris'* (service included), but it's usually just 5%. Elsewhere, a modest tip (10,000d or so) is always appreciated, but as a general rule, if a 10% tip amounts to almost nothing, don't bother tipping. If you hire a guide or driver to take you out of town, especially overnight, consider tipping them a few dollars. When visiting pagodas, it's customary to drop a small banknote into the donation box. Free musical performances and photo ops of colourful locals may also call for a monetary show of appreciation.

TOURIST INFORMATION

The government-run **Hapro Tourist Information Centre** (Map pp42-3, E4; ☎ 926 3366; 7 Pho Dinh Tien Hoang; 🕓 8am-10pm) is in the awkward large building overlooking the roundabout at the top of Hoan Kiem Lake. The friendly folks here can help with last-minute hotel reservations, package tours, visa issues and currency exchange. There's a 24-hour ATM on site, along with free information and maps.

TRAVELLERS WITH DISABILITIES

Hanoi is not particularly accommodating to the special needs of disabled travellers. The paucity of ramps is compounded by unruly traffic and crowded pavements. Still, Hanoians are often eager to be of help wherever possible. Many modern high-end hotels are wheelchair-accessible, and even some smaller hotels have lifts. **Disability Forum Vietnam** (☎ 933 1239; http://forum.wso.net; 33B Pham Ngu Lao, Hoan Kiem District) may be able to provide useful information.

>INDEX

See also separate subindexes for See (p158), Shop (p158), Eat (p159), Drink (p159) and Play (p159).

000 map pages

INDEX

000 map pages

INDEX

V

000 map pages